Y0-BXS-097

Effective Year-Round Bible Ministries

Edited by Margaret M. Self

The foreign language publishing of all Regal books is under the direction of GLINT. GLINT provides financial and technical help for the adaptation, translation and publishing of books in more than 85 languages for millions of people worldwide.

For more information write: GLINT, P.O. Box 6688, Ventura, CA 93006.

© Copyright 1980 by Regal Books
All rights reserved

Published by Regal Books
A Division of G/L Publications
Ventura, California 93006

Printed in U.S.A.

Library of Congress Catalog Card No. 80-52962
ISBN 0-8307-0751-4

Contents

How to Use This Book

First—Read, "Why Have a Special Bible Ministry?" Also, read the chapters describing each Bible ministry suggested in this book.

Second—After you and your committee have decided on a particular Bible ministry, study the chapters entitled, "Choosing Your Bible Study Curriculum," "Recruiting Your Staff," "Training Your Staff" and "Publicizing Your Program." To be sure you're allowing adequate time for each of these important steps, use the "Bible Ministries Countdown Schedule" in Part V.

Third—Read the "Following-Up and Evaluating" chapter in this book. Adapt the suggestions to your particular Bible ministry so you're ready at the conclusion of your program to put these important processes into action.

And now you're ready to go!!

May the God of peace ...equip you with everything good for doing his will...work in us what is pleasing to him, through Jesus Christ (Heb. 13:20, 21).

Part I

Why Have A Special Bible Ministry?

"I had time for my students to really get involved in discussion."

"My students and I became well acquainted by working together for an extended time."

"By teaching each day, I felt I improved my teaching skills."

"Learning was really an enjoyable experience for the kids!"

"The thrill of leading a child to Christ was mine for the first time."

"I sensed I was a valued part of a Bible teaching ministry."

"I really enjoyed getting to know my fellow teachers."

These kinds of comments brought a smile to the face of the director of Christian education as he thumbed through the VBS evaluation sheets. "Well," he whispered to himself, "we must be doing something right!"

The "something right" for this or any church begins with a commitment to a goal. Scripture clearly points the way. *But the goal of our instruction is love from a pure heart and a good conscience and a sincere faith (see 1 Tim. 1:5). We proclaim him, admonishing and teaching every one with all wisdom, that we may present every one perfect in Christ (Col. 1:28).*

People of all ages need to know of God's unconditional love that offers forgiveness through Jesus Christ. They also need that love demonstrated again and again in ways they can understand. And then they must have opportunities to become equipped for the task to which they are called.

This broad scripturally-oriented goal logically translates into several specific objectives. First, Scripture admonishes leaders and teachers to become skilled in their task. *Do your best to present yourself to God as one approved, a workman who does not need to be ashamed and who correctly handles the word of truth* (2 Tim. 2:15). A church has an obligation to train a staff for ministry. Simply presenting a challenge is not enough. Equipping people to respond successfully to the challenge is also crucial. In addition, each leader and teacher needs opportunities *to grow in the grace and knowledge of our Lord and Savior Jesus Christ* (2 Pet. 3:18). As each staff member's spiritual life grows and matures, he or she will be increasingly responsive to God's love and to the leading of the Holy Spirit.

A second objective evolving from this goal is a commitment to *encourage one another and build each other up* (1 Thess. 5:11). *If one part* [of the Body of Christ] *suffers, every part suffers with it; if one part is honored, every part rejoices with it* (1 Cor. 12:26). Learning to care for one another helps Christians mature in Christ. Sharing one another's joys and sorrows can build bonds of love to each other and to Christ.

The third objective has to do with the church's commitment to reach out to those who are completely unaware of the gospel of God's love; to witness to them, to disciple them. Childhood is a crucial age to reach for Christ because of the tremendous amount of development taking place during these formative years. Attitudes and values that will last a lifetime are being molded. A close relationship with Christ and with loving Christian adults can build into a child a healthy sense of who he or she is and a positive view of others.

The church also has a responsibility to nurture the boys and girls, youth and adults who are currently part of the church fellowship. Enabling people of all ages to learn of the Lord Jesus to the extent that they take upon themselves His likeness must be the heart of each program. Your ministry will help students grow toward spiritual maturity if it includes comprehensive Bible study with lots of opportunities for exploring and discovering in God's Word, and if it gives firsthand experiences in putting God's Word into action.

Providing an opportunity for learners to share the gospel with others in terms of a mission outreach is another facet of a church's commitment. Students need to be educated concerning the mission work currently being supported by their church, then challenged to consider the Great Commission in relation to their own lives. *Therefore go and make disciples of all nations, baptizing them in the name of the Father and of the Son and of the*

Holy Spirit, and teaching them to obey everything I have commanded you (Matt. 28:19, 20).

A TIME FOR EVERYTHING

There is a time for everything, and a season for every activity under heaven (Eccles. 3:1).

Although the Bible ministries in this book can be conducted most of the year, summer is an ideal time to fulfill the commitments so clearly spelled out in Scripture. School vacation schedules make many professional schoolteachers available for a short-term assignment. Also, the lack of summer school programs in many areas gives students (and teachers) free time. Many working parents welcome the opportunity to have their children in a church-sponsored program.

The summer season makes possible the use of facilities inappropriate during other months of the year. A park, beach, lake, the woods or other outdoor setting becomes a delightful environment conducive to a variety of activities. Weekday (in addition to Sunday) use of a church campus during the summer months demonstrates good stewardship of facilities and equipment. Spending time on the church grounds also gives learners a feeling of "belonging," an attitude transferable after the summer program concludes.

SELECTING OBJECTIVES

While the objectives stated in this chapter are viable, each church's leadership must think through the goals and objectives of their particular church before planning a Bible ministry. For example, if a church's first priority is outreach, then a Bible ministry must be selected and developed with that focus. If staff recruiting and training is of overriding importance, then its ministry needs to reflect that priority.

Another important step in selecting a new ministry is the evaluation of present ministries. Consider this idea:

1. Meet with key church leaders to think about ways you are currently involved in sharing God's love and His Word with people in the church and in the community.

2. On a chalkboard list five major categories of your church's work: worship, instruction, fellowship, evangelism, service.

3. Ask your committee members to list ways your church is now involved in each area. Indicate all opportunities your church offers for every age group.

Worship	Instruction	Fellowship	Evangelism	Service
Current Ministries				
Past Ministries				
Suggested New Ministries				

4. When you have listed everything the committee can think of in these categories, start a second list of all the kinds of ministries your church has used in past years. List them under one or more of these same headings.

5. Then list the name or brief description of any new ministries suggested in this book (see contents), as well as other ministries you have heard of or thought about doing.

6. Look at the first list to see where your church is NOW placing its priorities and resources. The second list will help you see the kinds of ministries you have had in past years. On the basis of these two listings you can see what your areas of emphases have been and where you are as a church.

7. Now you are ready to look ahead to possible new ways of accomplishing your objectives. Briefly outline the ministries described in this book. Look at each one in terms of the benefits it provides. Ask, "Does this ministry help us accomplish our objectives?"

Then compare each of these ministries with your chart of current programs. Which of these Bible ministries would help fill an existing gap? Which ones would be supplemental to your current program? Which ones would overlap present efforts? Do any of the new ministries offer a more effective ministry than some current programs?

As you make your selection, be aware of practical considerations, such as facilities, personnel, transportation and finances. Think in terms of which programs will strengthen your church's ministry to people of all ages. Also, consider community factors, such as school sessions, seasonal emphases and employment patterns. Be realistic in assessing both opportunities and difficulties. However, avoid letting possible problems deter you from responding to the full limit of your church's resources.

Stretch your faith and accept the challenge of expanding your summer ministries. Remember, *I have placed before you an open door that no one can shut* (Rev. 3:8).

Where and when will you have your Bible ministry?

Location Factors	Dates	Times
	VBS	
Was your church facility crowded last year or was there room to grow?	5, 6, 7, 10 days? Check records for previous programs.	*Morning:* 9:00 or 9:30 to 11:30 or 12:00.
Facilities should be appropriate to age group.	Check church calendar and summer school dates; church family vacations.	*Afternoon:* 1:00 to 3:30 or 4:00 (need rest periods for younger children).
Recreation rooms in condominiums, apartments, industrial park, factory, businesses.	Just after public school closes or just before it begins in fall are often good times.	*All day:* Bible learning in the morning, field trip or recreation in the afternoon.
Community hall.	When is a facility available?	*Split session:* (some in morning, some in afternoon) can ease crowding of facility; lets young people help out *and* have Bible study time.
Scout house.		
Y.M.C.A.		
Private schools.		Permits young children to attend in morning, school age in afternoon.
Retirement communities.		

Location Factors	Dates	Times
Vacant storefront. Parks.		Hot weather areas: try 3:00 to 6:00 P.M.
See VBS section.	**EVENING VBS** Every night for 1-2 weeks; twice a week for 5 weeks; once a week all summer. Check family schedules; summer school; camp. See VBS section.	6:30 or 7:00 to 9:00 P.M. (don't run too late).
A home with casual landscaping and enough space for 2-3 groups to work at the same time; grass for games, shaded area. No dangerous areas. Pets out of reach. Water and toilet in easy reach.	**BACKYARD BIBLE SCHOOL** Availability of home and hostess. Summer school, camp, etc. (see VBS section). Several backyard Bible schools can be scheduled on different dates.	2½-3 hours in the morning. Usually same as for morning VBS. Consider preferences of staff and needs of target audience. Use VBS schedule in teacher's book.
Park, private school.	**DAY CAMP** Every day for a week or once a week for 8-10 weeks.	Usually all day.

Location Factors	Dates	Times
Campground, private farm or ranch. Church grounds. Look for trees, grass, playground, other recreational facilities.	Consider the availability of site (may require reservations several months in advance). See VBS section for other factors in choosing dates.	Usually all day.
	FAMILY CAMP	
Conference center with adequate housing for families. No more than 2-3 hour drive. Has resident personnel (cooks, etc.). State or national park (for small church or group of families).	Availability of facility, personnel, speaker. Consider family vacations, summer school, sports programs, age-graded camps, VBS plans, vacation shut-down of local industry, local harvest periods. Set dates several months in advance.	(See scheduling suggestions in "Family Camp" chapter.)
	INTERGENERATIONAL	
See VBS section.	Every night for a week; once a week for several weeks.	6:30 or 7:00 to 9:00 P.M. (don't run too late).

Location Factors	Dates	Times
	HOLIDAY VBS	
Same as for regular VBS. Beach or resort area witnessing. Snow camp.	Holiday period (avoid actual holiday dates such as Easter or Christmas). See VBS section.	See VBS section.
	CHOIR TOUR	
Churches, nursing homes, convalescent homes, retirement centers, orphanages, schools for mentally or physically handicapped, prisons.	Same considerations as for VBS, plus availability of host churches and other facilities.	Start with weekends, work up to longer trips.
	OUTREACH	
Inner city or rural churches, Indian reservations, migrant camps, missions in Mexico. Campsites en route.	Begin planning 1-6 months ahead. Same considerations as VBS plus preference of personnel at host locations and availability of adult personnel to accompany young people.	Day by day, or two weeks or more.

Part II

What Kinds of Bible Ministries?

Deciding what kind of Bible ministry or ministries your church will sponsor is an important step. It should not be taken lightly. No ministry should be planned merely because "we've always done it." Rather, goals should be prayerfully established as suggested in Part I.

Selection of the target audience is also part of the goal-setting process. Do you want to minister to the people of the church, to the leaders, to children, to adults, to unchurched people in your neighborhood or your larger community, to groups of people with special needs? This question must be answered before you select your particular summer ministry.

The descriptions in this section will then help you determine which ministries will help you meet your goals and reach your target audience.

Chapter 1

Vacation Bible School

VBS is a special program traditionally built around Bible study and evangelistic outreach. One of the unique features of VBS is its flexibility in terms of age groupings, church and non-church participants, locations, staffing and program. VBS can involve groupings of children, youth and adults; it can include mostly church families or it can reach out into the neighborhood. It can provide in-depth Bible study opportunities to students already in the church; it can provide for the unchurched an opportunity to learn of God and His Word. It can be staffed by newly trained people who are teaching for the first time or it can be taught by high school and college age people who are challenged by its ministry. In some churches VBS is staffed by people who each year view this teaching opportunity as their special ministry. After having completed a successful teaching experience, this trained staff then becomes a rich resource for staffing other Christian education programs.

A successful VBS starts with careful and thoughtful planning—and this kind of planning starts early, as much as six months ahead. Turn to the "Bible Ministries Countdown Schedule" (see contents). Start checking off the completed items right away. Consistently use the schedule as you continue with your VBS preparation.

The first step in effective planning is to answer some basic questions:

"Why are WE conducting VBS this year?"
"What's OUR purpose?"
"Exactly what are WE trying to accomplish?"

OBJECTIVES FOR VBS

The traditional objectives are Bible teaching and outreach. You want to enrich the Bible knowledge and life response of your present Sunday School students. And you want to reach out to unchurched children, youth and adults in your community. Consider three factors as you decide on which objective to focus your VBS:

1. Study the enrollment cards from last year's VBS. Was the largest number of participants from your church? Should your emphasis be to reach "non-church" students?

2. Study the community around your church. Are you now effectively reaching that community for Christ? Would an evangelistic-oriented VBS, with special promotion in the community, help draw in students you are not now reaching?

3. Analyze your present church program. Do you have an effective outreach ministry? Would a special emphasis on evangelism through VBS strengthen that area of your church's Christian education program? Would an enriched Bible study program aid those children, youth and adults who attend your Sunday morning church school?

4. Another objective (in addition to Bible teaching and outreach) well worth considering is the training and spiritual growth of leaders and teachers. Would the five, seven or ten days of concentrated experience in VBS pay valuable dividends in in-service training for the staff? Would their time together help build loving and caring attitudes among them?

Whatever your decision, plan your VBS to complement, not compete with, the other programs in your church.

FACILITIES

As you think about what kind of VBS to plan, consider your facilities. Records (and remembering) from last year and the years before will help here. Were your facilities crowded with just the people from your congregation? Or did you have plenty of room—room to expand this year if you have an outreach VBS? Would split sessions (see "Dates and Times" section) help ease the crowding? Are the facilities appropriate to the age groups you are planning to include? Early childhood and children's classes usually work best in the rooms they use on Sunday morning. Teachers also appreciate the accessibility of materials and equipment in these rooms.

If folks who live in condominiums and apartments are your target group, then investigate the recreation rooms in these complexes. These facilities are usually available to residents free or for a small fee.

Consider a community hall, a Scout house or YMCA facility for VBS. Or perhaps the recreation room of an industrial park, factory or business; children could come and go with their parents and attend VBS while parents work or attend adult education classes.

Private schools, including Christian schools, are usually cooperative in giving permission for a VBS to be held in their building or on the grounds. A retirement community may be the ideal location if the seniors' group in your church is sponsoring a VBS. A vacant store in urban areas could be the site for VBS in a shopping center.

One church secured permission to use a part of a park each morning. A van loaded with appropriate equipment such as folding tables, ground covers, rope to define limits, and teaching materials drove to the park for each session. The schedule was planned for a different age level each week.

A church in Massachusetts used the church bus in another creative way—to solve a problem with seventh and eighth graders. The previous year, a small group of these students had been a disruptive element in VBS. A new plan emerged from concerned discussion and prayer. The associate pastor of the church and a young man willing to give a week of vacation time took over the junior high ministry and separated it from the other grade levels. They fitted out the church bus as a mobile classroom, with a portable chalkboard secured in a front seat and pictures taped to ceilings and walls.

Each day during the five-day school, the seventh and eighth graders rode the bus to an out-of-the-way location. The driving time was used for formation of teams and for checking of team points, looking over homework, and building team spirit. Then, when the bus stopped by the side of a dirt road, the two men, alternating days, guided students in a Bible study.

After the Bible study the bus rolled again, taking the students to a park for recreation—something different each day. This was followed by refreshments and then the drive back to the church.

This unusual mobile classroom salvaged the VBS experience for the junior-high-age students. There were no behavior problems; students did their homework and demonstrated their comprehension of the lesson material. Some received Christ; some joined Sunday School classes and youth groups who might not have done so otherwise. The church plans to repeat the ministry; and junior highers who went on to high school have asked to come back and help.

DATES AND TIMES

To determine the most appropriate dates to schedule your school, you will need to do the following:

1. Find out the dates of church camps, conferences and summer school in the community so that VBS will not conflict.

2. Review your VBS records from past years. Was a June VBS better attended than one in August? Holding VBS right after the close of school may enable children to attend before their families go on vacation. On the other hand, a VBS held just before school starts again allows for better follow-up and integration of new people into Sunday School classes.

3. Check with nearby churches to find out when they plan to have VBS. If possible, avoid duplication.

4. Talk to the people you want to involve. Find out when your potential staff members will be available (consider family vacations).

5. Consider the available dates of the facilities your VBS will require.

Once you've decided on your dates, you can consider the time. Will you offer a morning, afternoon, or all-day VBS? Here are some things to think about:

Morning is the traditional time for VBS. Mornings are cooler and people are fresher then. Usually a morning school lasts two-and-a-half to three hours: from 9:00 or 9:30 to 11:30 or 12:00.

Afternoon schools are usually scheduled from 1:00 to 3:30 or 4:00. However, this time schedule will interfere with nap time for the younger children. If you choose an afternoon VBS, you may need to provide a mid-afternoon rest period.

Another option is to have VBS for younger children in the morning and for school-age children in the afternoon. Such a split session will help if your facilities are limited in teaching space. It also enables young people to serve as helpers and teachers at one session, and to have their own Bible learning time during the other.

An all-day school can provide opportunities for Bible learning in the morning and field trips or other recreational activities in the afternoon.

If hot weather is a problem in your area, and if the public schools in your community have summer sessions, a school scheduled for 3:00 to 6:00 might be best.

ALTERNATIVE IDEAS FOR VBS

A ministry on wheels. Build a pushcart from used lumber. Paint it with bright colors and top it with a beach umbrella. Form a team consisting of a leader and two or three assistants. (High schoolers trained for your Bible ministry may enjoy this kind of work.) Plan half-hour sessions, to be repeated. Include puppet plays, Bible stories, simple crafts, refreshments, songs, and finger-fun poems. Schedule the pushcart ministry for two or three hours each day over a two-week period. Follow a route publicized in advance; or simply stop the cart and present the program whenever a group of children shows interest. Record names, phone numbers, and addresses of children for later follow-up.

Bilingual VBS. If your community has a large non-English-speaking population, consider a bilingual VBS. High school or college students who are studying the target language or who speak it at home, can prepare publicity materials and serve as teachers' aides to assist the children.

If you have a refugee population speaking a language that no one in the church knows, consider hiring a member of that population who is fluent in English as well as the other language. Let this person help prepare publicity materials and serve as an interpreter. This may provide a "port of entry" into the church for the interpreter as well as the children.

At the closing program of the ministry, arrange for one or two adults who speak both languages to be at the displays. Provide outreach materials in both English and the target language for parents. (Check church supplier for materials well in advance. Some may need to be ordered.)

For the closing program, show slides (taken during the early part of the week) of children participating in each part of the day's program. Be sure each child appears in several slides. Narrate in both languages. Emphasize the Bible learning aspect of each segment of the schedule.

Recycle VBS. Reuse the time and effort your staff spent in planning and training. During the summer months repeat your VBS in different locations. Begin by asking your pastor and church's mission committee for the names of rural or inner city churches where no summer program is planned because of personnel limitations or lack of funds. Offer the services and experience of your staff. The cost of such an outreach is minimal, requiring only the replacement of student books and craft supplies.

EQUIPMENT AND SUPPLIES

Decide early the curriculum you will use (see contents for "Choosing Your Bible Study Curriculum"); also determine the craft project, refreshments, recreation and/or other activities. Then make a list (by department) of equipment and supplies you'll need. Include *everything* from teacher's book to crayons, tables and chairs to volleyballs and paper cups. Some supplies and equipment, of course, you will already have, but make sure they will actually be available at the appropriate time. The rest will need to be purchased or donated by church members.

RECRUITING

Start your recruiting early (about four months in advance) after you have read "Recruiting Your Staff" (see contents). You will need a director, co-director, department leaders, teachers, registrar/secretary; and coordinators for missions, supplies, crafts, refreshments, transportation, finance and publicity. You'll also need a person who has first-aid knowledge and experience. ("Recruiting Your Staff" includes job descriptions.)

STAFF TRAINING

Start your training program about three months before VBS begins (see contents for "Training Your Staff"). You will need samples of all Bible teaching materials and craft supplies for teachers and helpers to use at training sessions.

SCHEDULING

Look over the schedules on the following pages in terms of your particular situation. Note that Bible study occurs early in the program; that there are frequently alternating periods of quiet and active participation; that learners have involvement activities as soon as they arrive; that time is allowed for moving from one activity to another.

HERE'S A WAY TO SCHEDULE
EARLY CHILDHOOD VBS

Recommended Time Schedules	Daytime 3 Hours	Evening 2 Hours
BIBLE LEARNING ACTIVITY TIME	**50 min.**	**35 min.**
Creative Art • Blocks/Carpentry • Listening Corner • God's Wonders • Game Table • Home Living—A teacher assigned to each area guides activity and uses suggested conversation to relate activity to Bible learning aim. Children are free to move from one activity area to another.	40 min.	30 min.

Helping—Teachers guide children in putting away   10 min.   5 min.
learning activity materials.

TOGETHER TIME   **35 min.**   **25 min.**
Sharing—Teachers and children gather in one group   15 min.   10 min.
for music and sharing of Bible learning activities.
Bible Story/Activity—Children go to Bible story class-   20 min.   15 min.
es of 6 to 8 children per teacher. Teacher presents
visualized Bible story, then guides children in use of
student books.

PLAYTIME   **45 min.**   **20 min.**
Game—Teachers guide children in outdoor play activi- 20 min.   ——
ties.
Wash-Up/Snack/Rest   25 min.   20 min.

LISTENING TIME   **15 min.**   **15 min.**
Child Experience Story—Leader guides several activ-
ity songs, then tells a story to relate Bible teaching/
learning aim to children's everyday experience.

FUN-TO-DO TIME   **35 min.**   **25 min.**
Craft—Children return to class groups to complete a   15 min.   15 min.
craft project.
Music Fun/Good-Byes—As time allows, children work 20 min.   10 min.
at table activities until parents come. Teachers guide
children in these activities: *Puzzles • Pegs and
Pegboards • Salt/Flour Dough • Books*

LEADER'S AND TEACHERS' TIME
Clean-Up—Teachers straighten and put away materials and equipment.
Evaluation/Planning—Leader and teachers make
plans for tomorrow. Conclude with prayer.

HERE'S A WAY TO SCHEDULE
CHILDREN'S VBS (GRADES 1-6)

Recommended Time Schedules	*Daytime* *3 Hours*	*Evening* *2 Hours*
EXPLORING GOD'S WORD	**75 min.**	**45 min.**
Building Readiness—As child arrives he chooses activity that introduces lesson's Bible teaching aim.	20 min.	10 min.
Bible Study—Teacher leads permanent group of 6-8 children. Teacher presents Bible story; also guides Bi- ble memorization.	30 min.*	20 min.

Living God's Way—Teacher guides children in completing student book, applying Bible truth to life.   25 min.*   15 min.

SHARING   15 min.   15 min.
Teachers and children gather in one group for music and sharing.

RECREATION/REFRESHMENTS   45 min.   25 min.
Teachers guide children in outdoor play activities.   30 min.   15 min.
All share light refreshments.   15 min.   10 min.

NATURE/CRAFTS   30 min.   20 min.
Children work on craft project or nature study.

PRAISE TIME   15 min.   15 min.
Teachers and children gather in one group for concluding worship and sharing.

Shorten this time for younger children. Use extra time for Bible learning activities.

HERE'S A WAY TO SCHEDULE YOUTH VBS

Recommended Time Schedules	Daytime 3 Hours	Evening 2 Hours
WELCOME/FELLOWSHIP Teachers informally greet each student.	15 min.	10 min.
BIBLE EXPLORATION To help accomplish the Bible learning aim, teachers guide students in:	70 min.	50 min.
Introductory Activities	10 min.	10 min.
Worship	10 min.	10 min.
Bible Study	50 min.	30 min.

Divide students in small groups (8-10 students); and then reassemble in one large group. For each activity choose a large or small group setting.
For example, introductory activities use large group; worship, small groups; Bible study, large, then small groups. Vary these arrangements from day to day.

RECREATION/CRAFTS   50 min.   25 min.
Students complete craft project or play games.   35 min.   25 min.
Refreshments available during time for recreation and   15 min.   ——
crafts or immediately following.

ADAPTING THESE SCHEDULES

These recommended schedules are guidelines to assist leaders and teachers in planning a balanced learning program to meet the needs of each age level. As you make necessary adaptations, consider:

Curriculum—Specific courses may suggest variations in order to accomplish particular Bible learning aims.

Facilities—Small, crowded rooms may require shorter time blocks to avoid over-stimulation. Or shared use of outdoor play areas may make it necessary to adjust schedules. For example, while one department has recreation, another is having crafts.

Age groupings—When wide age spans are grouped together, interest in sit-still-and-listen activities is often difficult to maintain. If you must group together children of widely varying ages, allow additional time for small group activities where individual differences can be more easily met.

Activities—The amount of time required for activity or craft will vary according to learners' interest and ability. Adjust the time schedule from day to day to accommodate these variations.

PREREGISTRATION

Communicating early and often to the people in the church is an essential part of a successful VBS. The more students you can sign up ahead of time, the calmer the first day of VBS will be.

A "kiosk," portable VBS booth (see sketch) provides a focal point for giving information, preregistering students, posting eye-catching displays, creating interest, and so on.

The booth can be used year after year and is well worth the investment.

If a booth is impossible in your situation, provide an attractively decorated table.

Set up your booth or table on Easter Sunday and Mother's Day to register people who don't attend church regularly. Then, for at least three weeks before the start of VBS, continue with registrations.

Use registration cards (available from VBS suppliers). Over the corner of each card put a small piece of colored tape or a self-stick label (a different color for each department) to help you quickly classify the students. Use the same color on the door of the department and on name tags for teachers and students to help you locate strays and to help the students know where they belong.

See "Publicizing Your Program" in this book for suggestions on canvassing areas of your community personally and by mail.

Make a kiosk from a large appliance carton to create interest in VBS. Cut doors in the carton in a variety of shapes and sizes. (See sketch.) Paint the entire carton with brightly colored poster paint. On the outside of each door letter WHO? WHAT? WHEN? WHERE? and HOW?, one word per door.

Inside each door tape paper on which you have lettered appropriate information. See sketch. For example, inside the WHO? door, letter the names (or display pictures) of students who will be attending VBS. Include teachers' names also. Inside the WHERE? and WHEN? doors letter dates and location of VBS. Inside the WHAT? door, give information about special VBS features, such as field trips, etc. Decorate the box with color designs and VBS theme poster, GOOD NEWS! JESUS LOVES YOU.

On Sunday place your eye-catching kiosk near a well-traveled area where it will be readily seen. Change the WHO? WHAT? and HOW? information each week to sustain interest.

CLOSING PROGRAM

A closing program, picnic or open house is a traditional way to conclude VBS. This opportunity allows students to share with their families what they have learned at VBS. "Closing the Program" in this book provides a variety of suggestions.

EVALUATION AND FOLLOW UP

Begin reading "Following-up and Evaluating" (see contents). First give thanks and praise to the Lord for what He did, then express your thanks to those who worked so hard to share Christ through VBS.

Chapter 2

Evening Vacation Bible School

An evening Bible school works out well in many cases. Such a school usually goes from 6:30 or 7:00 to 9:00 P.M. An evening school will enable employed people to be included as teachers or in other roles. There are at least three ways to set up such a school.

1. For youth or older children meeting at homes or at church. The information and suggestions for daytime Bible school apply. One church had an evening school for teens at a home with a good-sized backyard and a pool. Bible classes were conducted inside the home, with crafts and recreation (including swimming) taking place outside.

2. For the entire family, with separate classes for the various age groups, including adults. Regular VBS curriculum may be used, just as in a daytime school.

3. For the entire family with an intergenerational approach. In this type of school, all family members aged four and above meet and study together. There may be one or more segments during each evening when children and adults are separated, but even then the material they study is coordinated so that when they get together again, they are sharing from a common background. One example, one curriculum available for intergenerational study is the *Family Values Workshop* (Gospel Light Publications, 1979), which provides five sessions, with leader's guide and

family guides. Gospel Light's *Adventure Through the Bible* take-home papers also provide valuable resources. Each paper presents a Bible story plus family and kids-only activities.

In planning an evening VBS, you will need to recognize that it may attract fewer unchurched people from the community than a daytime schedule. However, an evening school provides the opportunity to help families establish and maintain a Christian family life-style. Also, evening VBS can involve persons who work during the day.

Your planning, recruiting, and training will need to cover the same bases as for a daytime school (see contents for appropriate chapters). Remember to include staff persons for adult classes if you offer them. Remember also to provide nursery care for the youngest children and babies.

You will also need to determine your schedule. Some churches have successful schools that meet every evening for one or two weeks. Others have good response to a twice-a-week evening schedule for five weeks. Another possibility is one evening a week for the entire summer.

Check with families to determine the times those interested will be available. Also check summer school and camp schedules and the other information suggested in the VBS chapter.

The sample schedules in the section on daytime VBS include suggestions for ways to allocate the time in an evening school.

Chapter 3

Backyard Bible School

If outreach is one of your Bible ministry goals, consider taking VBS to the children, right where they are in their own neighborhood. Many younger children, or those who do not attend church, may feel more comfortable in the familiar surroundings of a neighbor's yard than at the church or at a day camp site. A backyard school provides ideal opportunities for neighborhood outreach and evangelism. Also, both children and teachers enjoy learning about God in an informal, natural environment. Bible schools in a home setting provide a way to get around transportation problems and inadequate church facilities. Since fewer adults are involved, these schools allow for increased flexibility as to time schedule. Many churches and individuals find these schools are both fun and productive in ministering to children.

FACILITIES

Use postal zip codes to divide your community into zones. In each zone, locate church members who have a suitable outdoor area such as a backyard, covered porch or patio, or carport. Visit each available location personally to determine its suitability. Choose "casually" landscaped yards with enough space for two or three small groups to work at the same time. A grassy spot for games and a shaded area are important. Swimming pools, fish ponds, dogs and other pets and destructible plantings need to be out of reach. Check what's next door, too. An otherwise-suitable backyard may have neighbors with a large, noisy, frightening dog or other distraction.

Water and toilet facilities should be easily accessible. The house interior should be considered "off limits" except for toilet facilities. Tables and chairs are helpful but not essential. Have children sit on the grass or a blanket; use magazines or cardboard for lap desks.

When you and your committee select yards for Bible school, consider areas where you have a concentration of church families. Plan to have one age-group department at each home—all kindergartners in one backyard, for example. Or, if necessary, all preschool children (prekindergarten and kindergarten together) can be in one yard, and all early elementary age (primary, middler) in another yard.

Another way of grouping is to have ungraded schools in widespread neighborhoods. Plan so that children are grouped by age for small Bible study activities. The size of the yard will largely determine the size and grouping of each backyard school.

THE CHILDREN

Ten to fifteen children can work comfortably in most backyards. A very large yard may accommodate up to twenty children. Keep the school small to allow for ease of operation and personal contact with each student. Ages of children should be limited to four years through fourth grade (the most recently completed grade). Older children are better served through other Bible ministries described in this book.

Give host families and other interested people flyers to use in canvassing the neighborhood and church for children ages four through the fourth grade. Talk personally to parents, informing them of your plans, calendar dates and the time for arrival and departure each day. While some children from your church will attend, you will likely have a majority of non-church neighborhood children. (For suggestions for enlisting children's attendance, see "Publicizing Your Program" in this book.)

Preregister as many children as possible so you can adequately plan for age-level needs. Divide children into age-level classes of equal size such as four- and five-year-olds, first and second graders, and third and fourth graders. Assign one teacher to each class group.

Establish basic guidelines for acceptable behavior. Make rules simple; give clear instructions the first day. Inform children of boundaries, off-limit areas and use of equipment and materials. Keep your expectations for their behavior realistic. Understand that children in an outdoor setting will be more exuberant and active than they would be indoors.

THE TEACHING TEAM

There are three major areas of responsibility in backyard schools. These tasks are assigned to the leader, the teachers and the hostess.

The *leader* directs all large-group sessions and assists teachers during small-group activities. She or he is responsible for all organizational matters and planning.

One *teacher* is needed for each six to eight children (use the smaller number if your group is predominantly four- to six-year-olds). Assign each teacher one age-level group for the duration of the school.

The *hostess* is usually the one who has opened her home and yard. She is responsible for welcoming children, preparing and serving refreshments and caring for individual needs (comforting crying child, providing first aid, assisting children to restrooms, etc.). She may need some help; teenagers are a natural choice. This is the sort of thing they are glad to do, and can do well.

Additional staff can include a recreation leader and a baby-sitter. Young people are effective in these areas. Workers with children under age four appreciate a baby-sitter who can care for their child in the house while they are involved in teaching.

(For guidance in recruiting and training your staff, read "Recruiting Your Staff" and "Training Your Staff" in this book.)

DATES AND SCHEDULE

Because backyard schools involve small groups, setting the dates for the school is simpler than for large programs. The time need only be convenient for hostess, staff and the children. Even when one church schedules many backyard schools, they need not all be in session simultaneous.

Allow two and one-half to three hours for each daily session. Consider morning for these sessions, for the children are fresh and the weather is usually more comfortable.

Backyard Bible school can follow the VBS schedule suggested in teachers' books. It isn't necessary to have a closing program. Instead, plan an early evening open house as an opportunity to bring families together to share the experiences of the school and to see the learning activities and completed crafts.

THE CURRICULUM

The greatest challenge in a backyard school results from the variety of children's ages. Making appropriate adaptations in your teaching materials is an essential first step to children's effective learning. A practical approach is to use a Primary VBS course with the following adaptations:

1. Follow the basic time schedule suggested; however, shorten large group times to accommodate younger children's brief attention span.

2. Conduct all small group activities by age-level (early childhood) and grade-level (children). When choices are suggested in the teacher's manual, select the activity most appropriate for each age group. For example, activities suggested for one day may be: painting, frieze, and song chart. After reading the activity instructions, you may find the four- and five-year-olds capable only of the painting project. First and second graders can easily work on the frieze. Assign the song chart to the third and fourth graders (because of their reading abilities). On subsequent days, repeat an activity fours and fives especially enjoyed (for increased learning and enjoyment) as other age groups continue work on their projects.

3. While older students work on student books, provide an alternate activity for non-readers. Effective options include:
- Guide children in looking at picture books related to lesson aim.
- Take a discovery walk to find things God has made.
- Enjoy a brief quiet time of listening to music or neighborhood sounds.
- Guide children in using Bible story visuals to retell the story.

4. Evaluate the craft kits to determine difficulty level. Consider these suggestions:
- Provide early childhood craft kits for younger children.
- Give extra assistance to younger children.
- Assign older child to work with younger child (requires mixing class groups during this time period).
- Select an alternate activity from *158 Things to Make* or *Easy to Make Crafts (for children ages 3-11).* (See Part V chapter in this book.)

5. Be alert to the needs of your particular group and adapt suggestions accordingly. Daily evaluation by your staff is essential in successfully tailoring any curriculum to your children's needs and interests.

Use the outdoor setting to build relationships with each child by sharing discoveries of things God has made. The quality of these relationships is vital to your efforts in introducing children to the Lord Jesus.

Each day gather your staff together for prayer. Ask the Lord Jesus to help you be alert to opportunities to express His love to children and parents.

Chapter 4

Day Camp

Day camp is an outdoor activity and learning program just one step removed from resident camping. It offers the experiences of resident camp without the prolonged absence from home. Day campers eat with their families in the morning and the evening, and sleep at home. They usually spend from 9:00 in the morning to 3:00 or 4:00 in the afternoon at day camp. There they participate in camp-type activities such as nature walks, recreation, crafts, and small-group Bible study.

Day camp provides an opportunity to discover new and wonderful things about this world God has created and called "good." Making these kinds of discoveries does not always necessitate going into the country. Day camp can help increase children's awareness of their own city environment. In groups of not more than ten children, walk through your community to smell food aromas, observe ways love is being shown (in day care centers, convalescent homes, by community helpers and families), observe flowers and vegetables in front yards and even plant growth in sidewalk cracks.

Whether you transport boys and girls to a country environment or stay on your church campus, a day camp schedule allows unique opportunities for alert leaders to guide children in enlarging their view of their world and discovering and applying Bible truths in that world. *Talk about [God's commands] when you sit at home and when you walk along the road, when you lie down and when you get up* (Deut. 6:7).

Day camping also provides a setting for developing significant relationships between counselors and campers. Hikes, nature studies, and camp crafts augment the Bible exploration time, an important part of each day's activities. A counselor with no more than eight or ten campers can establish a close relationship with these boys and girls in a day camp situation.

Day camp is especially popular with middlers and juniors—grades 3-6. They thrive on the outdoor aspects of the program. For many the day camp experience is a good transition from VBS to resident camp.

Junior highs also enjoy a modified day camp experience. Let them help plan the program, including the kinds of recreational activities they especially enjoy.

A well-planned day camp program offers many benefits to your church and its children. The fun of day camp will encourage children to bring their unchurched friends, providing a natural opportunity for evangelism and outreach. Daily contact with other children in the camp situation will help build important Christian-living attitudes and skills.

Bible study can take on new meaning in the out-of-doors, for the setting of most Bible stories was outdoors. Children quickly and naturally develop an appreciation of God's creation through firsthand experiences. They readily learn to help keep their environment clean and to leave the natural beauty unspoiled.

CHOOSE A SITE

A park, campground or other public recreational facility, a private farm or ranch are all desirable locations for a day camp. Another possibility is the campus of a Christian school associated with your church or another church in the area, or possibly even another type of private or public school, if the campus has grass, trees, playgrounds and other recreational facilities. Even your church grounds may serve. If the property lacks needed facilities, plan daily field trips to locations where nature paths, hiking trails and other recreational activities are available.

If you want a location other than your church, look for one not more than thirty minutes driving distance from the church. Start looking early (three to six months ahead), because good places are filled quickly. When you sign up for a particular site, find out what insurance you will need for your day campers. Have several possible dates in mind when you start looking for a site, so you can make adjustments to get just the place you want.

Make a checklist to be sure you have considered all the points for and against each location:

1. Distance from church (should be within a thirty-minute drive).
2. Protected area (a place out of the rain or hot sun to use for crafts even on pleasant days).
3. Type of terrain (no dangerous trails, cliffs, swampy areas or abundance of poison oak or ivy).
4. Trails (easy trails for nature walks).
5. Adequate water supply.
6. Restroom facilities.
7. Place for swimming or wading, with a place where children can change clothes. (Or plan to use the church van or bus for clothes-changing.)
8. Size (places for several small groups to meet without disturbing each other; also a place for the entire group to meet together).
9. Location (some privacy from the public).

ESTABLISH TIMES AND BUDGET

You have selected the location. Now it's time to think about dates and scheduling. In some cases, in order to get the location you wanted, you will have accepted the date it is available. In other cases you will have more freedom to decide. Working within the options that are open to you, consider the following possible plans: Some day camps meet daily for one or two weeks. This provides continuity for the learning process. Other camps meet once a week for five or ten weeks. In this plan, middlers might attend on Tuesdays, juniors on Wednesdays, and junior highs on Thursdays. This plan loses some benefits of continuity but gains the advantage of working with just one age group at a time.

Plan a detailed camp budget as early as possible. Include transportation, insurance, supplies (including curriculum and crafts), site rental, promotion; also any food, refreshments and awards you plan to provide. Some churches write the cost into their annual budgets.

You may decide to charge each camper a fee. The fee may cover the entire cost of the camper, or it might be a token payment to help campers feel that they have a part in maintaining the day camp. Consider offering a discount to parents with more than one child in camp and establishing "camperships" for those unable to pay. Individuals and adult Bible classes in your church may want to participate by contributing to day camp scholarship funds. (Be sure that the children receiving "campership" funds write notes of thanks, telling the donors what camp meant to them.) The church may wish to launch a fund-raising effort that will benefit all day campers. For example, a paper drive is fairly simple to manage, and most people are able and willing to bring their newspapers, sacked in grocery bags. Young people can be responsible for stacking them and for loading them into a vehicle for transportation to a redemption site. (Other suggestions for providing funds are in the "Finance Coordinator" section of the chapter on "Recruiting Your Staff.")

DETERMINE STAFFING REQUIREMENTS

(For recruiting guidelines, read the chapter "Recruiting Your Staff.")

Choose staff members who share your concern for the spiritual emphasis of your day camp, and who also have experience or can be trained in their specific job responsibilities.

You may want to pay the key leaders something for their services, thereby providing job opportunities for your church's young people, vacationing school teachers, or others in need of a financial boost. Be sure you include the cost of all such salaries in your budget planning.

The *camp director* is the key to a successful day camp, so choose him or her carefully. The director is in charge of the entire day camp operation, including the advance planning and the actual operation of the camp itself. Select a person who understands the age group that will attend the camp, who has a camping background, and who can effectively supervise a staff. (The camp director's responsibilities are similar to those of the VBS director described in the chapter on "Recruiting Your Staff.")

Provide a *counselor* and an *assistant counselor* for each eight to ten campers. These counselors will be with their groups constantly during the camp program. High school and college young people make excellent assistants, and occasionally an outstanding young person can serve effectively as a counselor. Counselors and assistants should be at least five years older than their campers.

Counselors and assistants supervise their groups' activities throughout the entire day. Their main responsibilities are guiding Bible study, student's book activities and memory work. Although specialist coordinators (crafts, recreation, missions) will work with the children in these activities, the counselors are always available to assist.

Your staff should include additional personnel, such as a *craft director,* missions coordinator, and *recreation leader.* Young people can serve as recreation assistants.

Also provide a *co-director* who is learning the job and who is committed to being director next year. (See "Recruiting Your Staff" for more suggestions regarding the co-director.)

Because nature study is such an important part of a day camp, recruit a *nature guide* to handle the nature walks and other related activities. The nature walks will help campers learn about the wonders of God's creation.

A cheerful, skilled *food crew* will do much to make your day camp a happy experience for everyone. Ask your campers to bring a sack lunch each day; provide a small carton of milk. (If any campers are allergic to milk, ask parents to provide an alternate drink.) The food crew stores campers' lunches until lunch time (in ice chests or coolers if possible); sets out lunches and milk cartons in time for lunch; cleans up after lunch; and sets out refreshments at other times of the day. You may want to provide a cookout once or twice during the day camp session. Young people, with adequate supervision, can serve as the food crew.

Other staff needs may include a *secretary, supply, publicity, finance* and *transportation coordinators.* If you use a swimming pool you will need a certified *lifeguard.* You will also need someone well-trained and certified in *first aid.* Provide a basic first-aid kit with bandages, antiseptic, sunscreen lotion, and a soothing lotion for sunburn.

TRAIN YOUR STAFF WELL

Use the training plan suggested in the chapter titled "Training Your Staff." In addition to the regular training sessions, you will want to take your staff to the campsite at least once before the first day camp session. With your staff, plan where each of the activities will take place. Avoid placing the Bible study classes in direct sun. Crafts and Bible study groups will need a place where wind will not be a problem. Be sure everyone knows what to do in case of rain. You may meet in a sheltered place at the campsite, or stay at church. If neither is possible, it may be necessary to tell the children not to come on rainy days.

Craft leaders will need to decide on appropriateness of craft projects in terms of campsite: Is water available for painting and clean-up? Will tables be needed or can campers work on plastic ground covers?

Nature leaders will provide nature walks and some nature crafts. Local YMCA, YWCA, Boy and Girl Scouts and similar organizations can give help in your specific locale. (See "Resources" for books on nature lore.)

PLAN FOR EQUIPMENT AND MATERIALS

An outdoor school requires some equipment and materials you would not ordinarily need. *Tables:* folding tables may be needed for registration and to hold craft supplies, students' books, refreshments and lunches. *Clothesline rope:* rope strung between trees can be used to hang maps, posters and other visual aids and to mark boundaries for special areas. *Ground Covers:* sheets of plastic (the size of trash bags) make adequate mats to lay on damp grass or dirt areas. Children sit and work on mats in lieu of tables. *Ice chests* or *coolers* to hold sack lunches and milk, and *thermos containers* for water, punch, coffee are convenient. *A flipchart* on rope strung between trees is a good outdoor substitute for chalkboard or overhead projector.

Bible learning materials for your supply list should include: students' Bible study books, materials for making crafts, maps, friezes, murals, etc. Counselors will work with the supply coordinator in collecting the supplies that are suggested in teachers' and leaders' manuals for each department.

Recruit help from the church at large in providing supplies such as pencils, craft materials and other items that can be donated.

PREREGISTER THE STUDENTS

Some communities limit the number of people using a campsite. Check this item carefully so that you will not over-register. (See chapter titled "Publicizing Your Program" for publicity and registration suggestions.) If you find that your camp is full and you have a waiting list, consider a second camp, or plan the once-a-week schedule described earlier.

As you register day camp students, also secure the parent's signature on a permission slip. (See contents for "Sample Permission Form.") This slip should grant you permission to transport the child from the church to camp and return. It should also give permission for the child to be given first aid by a nurse or doctor. Give parents an opportunity to comment on allergies, special diets, or medications needed by their children. For example, a child who is allergic to chocolate or who is on a sugar-free diet should not be offered candy; camp personnel should be alert to keep other children from tempting the dieting child. If a child takes medication, parents should give it to the camp director in the morning and the director or counselor should give it to the child at the appropriate time.

Make it clear to the children that they are to come in play clothes, and that day camping is an active outdoor experience. If swimming or wading is part of the program, ask campers to bring swim wear in waterproof bags.

Explain your rainy-day schedule (i.e., no camp on rainy days; or "camp" indoors at the church) in a letter to the parents. Give information about lunch—each child should bring his or her own. If you will have ice chests, say so. If not, suggest lunch items that can safely be held until noon (i.e. peanut butter or cheese sandwiches, fruit, fresh vegetables such as celery and tomatoes) and lunch items to avoid (mayonnaise, uncured luncheon meats). Specify the time the children will leave for and return from camp. Explain that the bus must leave at the designated time; punctuality is of great importance. Then adhere to this commitment.

PLAN A CHRIST-CENTERED PROGRAM

In all the fun and excitement that is a natural part of day camp, don't forget that this is primarily a spiritual ministry. Every part of the camping experience—including the recreation and other fun activities—influences the camper's life. Keep this spiritual emphasis constantly in mind without stifling the wholesome fun atmosphere of the camp. The natural setting gives you the opportunity to let children know that God *has shown kindness by giving you rain from heaven and crops in their seasons; he provides you with plenty of food and fills your hearts with joy* (Acts 14:17).

The Bible study curriculum you use does much to set the spiritual tone of your day camp. Biblically-sound VBS teaching and learning guidance is essential for the Bible learning activities of your camp.

Every day provides new opportunities for you and your day camp staff to reach out in Christian love to the campers. You will be very busy during camp, and it will be easy to forget that the campers are learning from your actions as well as your words. Pray that in all your activities God will help you reflect the Christ you want your campers to know and love as their Saviour and Lord.

Do not allow a rigid schedule to eliminate important individual counsel with campers. Encourage your group counselors to watch for campers who need some special personal attention. A puzzled expression or a revealing question may be the only clue a camper gives to indicate that he or she needs to spend a few moments alone with his or her counselor discussing important spiritual or personal matters. Counselors should be able to leave their groups with their assistant counselor for a few moments in order to handle this vital personal work. Other opportunities include one-to-one conversation over lunch or during the large group missions time—conversation that can lead to life-changing decisions and the beginning of a lifetime commitment to the Lord Jesus Christ.

Day camp is also a time for your campers themselves to reach out to others in Jesus' name. Encourage them to invite their friends to camp. Help them make the newcomers feel welcome. Sometime during each day's activities include a simple explanation of God's love for them and His plan for their becoming a member of God's forever family. For ways to include these vitally important concepts in your natural conversation, read "Leading a Child to Christ" in this book.

PLAN YOUR DAY CAMP SCHEDULE

Here is a typical daily schedule. Study this schedule carefully with your staff several weeks before your day camp begins. Make whatever modifications you believe are necessary. (Breaks between activities allow time for restroom visits and washing up.)

9:00—Meet at church

On the first day register campers as they arrive. Be sure to register each newcomer who comes on succeeding days. Make sure each one gives you a permission slip signed by parent or guardian.

After registration each morning, lead the campers into a bus for transportation to the day camp site. Make sure leaders have a list of all campers who enter the bus so no one is left behind at the end of the day. The director should take the permission slips to the site, in case they are needed in an emergency.

During the drive to the camp site divide the campers into three teams. Let them choose appropriate names, such as "Lions," "Leopards" and "Tigers" or "Palominos," "Arabians" and "Pintos." If more than one age is attending day camp divide the campers according to age, since this division is the basis for Bible learning, craft and recreational activities.

Subdivide each team into groups of eight to ten campers. Assign a counselor and assistant to each group. Each child stays with his or her group throughout each day.

9:30— Arrive at camp

Have all counselors leave the bus first and station themselves side-by-side a few yards away. Then allow the campers to line up behind their counselors. While in this formation open the day with prayer, flag salutes and any necessary announcements.

Then have the assistant counselors collect their teams' lunches. Be sure each camper's name is on his or her lunch. (Be prepared with pens to write names on sack lunches; use grease pencil or self-stick labels for lunch boxes.) If possible, provide ice chests to keep the food fresh. Then counselors lead their groups to the day's first activity.

9:45-10:45—Bible learning activities

Follow your VBS Bible study curriculum for the first part of the day's program. Adapt the class schedule indicated in the teacher's manuals if changes are required to fit the overall day camp program. Each counselor guides his or her group in Bible study with students using their workbooks, Bibles and Bible memory work activities.

On the first day explain that the members of each group will do everything together as a group. "No one will be left out of any activity. Each of us cares about everyone else in the group. No one may leave the group at any time without permission."

10:55-11:40—Team activities

Following the Bible learning time in which the campers are divided into small groups, each team assembles for the first of three team activity periods.

During this first period Team 1 meets at the craft center, where the *craft director* has prepared craft projects. Each group works on its craft projects under the direction of its group counselor and the craft director.

Team 2 meets at the nature center during the first activity period. There the *nature leader* briefly discusses the purpose of the nature time. He or she may take the team on a short nature walk, guiding campers in identifying and discussing interesting plants, animals and topographical/geological characteristics. Encourage the campers to watch for specific items and potential craft materials such as twigs, leaves, pinecones and seedpods.

Team 3 spends its first activity period at the recreation center. There the *recreation director,* assisted by the group counselors and assistant counselors, leads the campers in a variety of activities, such as team and individual games, relay races, and instruction in skills such as archery or horseback riding. (See chapter entitled "Resources," the section on "Camp Games, Crafts, Creative Activities.") If a lake or swimming pool is available, allow swimming on certain days under the watchful eye of the lifeguard. Explain and then require all to conform to water safety rules. (Inform the campers a day ahead, so they can bring swim suits and towels in waterproof bags.)

11:50-12:30—Lunch

Campers gather by groups with their counselors at the lunch center where they eat their lunches together.

12:40-1:25—Team activities

Repeat the team activities as described above. Rotate the teams, so that Team 1 is at the nature center, Team 2 at recreation and Team 3 at crafts. Allow ten minutes between each kind of activity for teams to move from one area to the next.

1:35-2:20—Team activities

Team 1 moves to recreation, Team 2 to crafts, and Team 3 to the nature center. Be sure that small groups stay together, that the counselors work closely with their groups and are responsible for each of their campers at all times.

2:30-3:05—Fellowship/missions period

Have each team meet separately for fun songs, stunts and skits, fellowship and the missions emphasis. If your camp is small and includes only one age group, you may want to bring all three teams together for this period.

3:05-3:20—All together

Use this concluding time for brief moments of worship. Add a special outdoors or nature emphasis wherever possible. Then make any necessary final announcements and board the buses or cars for transportation back to the church.

4:00—Arrival at church

Counselors remain with their campers until campers are called for by parents. Have on hand some equipment for quiet activities (puzzles, games, books) to occupy campers while they wait for rides. Make sure staff people understand that they *must* wait until the last child is picked up.

PLAN YOUR CLOSING PROGRAM

An interesting closing program is a good way to establish contact with the parents and families of your day campers. Invite the parents to a special wiener roast on the last night of your day camp session. Take them on a short nature walk, and allow their children to share interesting things about the natural camp setting. Display the childrens' craft projects. If time permits, include camper-parent relay games. Then allow the campers to share some Bible lessons and verses which had special meaning to them during camp. Conclude with a campfire sing time.

EVALUATE AND FOLLOW-UP

An effective day camp is not over when the closing program is concluded. Now is the time to evaluate and begin plans for next year. (See chapter entitled "Following-Up and Evaluating.") Before you forget the details, write down the ideas you feel should be considered next year and note those parts of the program which should be modified or omitted.

Keep in touch with the campers. Give their names and addresses to the appropriate Sunday School departments for follow-up.

Send a word of appreciation to the members of your staff. Think back over the entire activity. It was work, but wasn't it worth it all? Think of the young people that the Lord touched through you. Praise Him! God is good!

> *Praise be to the Lord God, the God of Israel,*
> *who alone does marvelous deeds.*
> *Praise be to his glorious name forever;*
> *may the whole earth be filled with his glory*
> (Ps. 72:18, 19).

Chapter 5
Family Camp

A family camp provides an opportunity for families to live together in a relaxed, informal atmosphere of Christian fellowship and oneness. Separate activities for various ages during part of the day help meet the needs and interests of each family member. Yet the overall program is designed to strengthen family relationships. Families live together, eat their meals together, worship together, enjoy a family-oriented project together and are encouraged to play together during the afternoon recreational period. Some churches are also experimenting with having intergenerational study and activity times, allowing families to spend even more time together in constructive activities, while still recognizing the need for some times of separate age-group activities. See chapter on "Intergenerational Programs" for further information on intergenerational study.

At family camp, working and playing together in the out-of-doors helps bridge the gaps that often separate family members. Children and parents get to know one another in new ways. Love and trust begin to bloom. A whole new style of family life may result.

Families that live and play side by side inevitably grow closer to one another. Thus a family camp can help build stronger relationships within the church family as well.

Without many of the distractions of home, job and other everyday responsibilities, individual family members are free to open themselves to God and His Word. Concentrated Bible study and Christian-living classes, inspiring speakers and counselors and devotional times help individual family members grow. Growing individuals help families and churches grow.

A successful family camp begins with careful planning well in advance. First, decide who in the church is responsible for the camp. The idea of a family camp will probably begin with the board of Christian education, who should appoint a family camp director. The board and the director should clearly define the reasons for having a family camp. What are the major needs you see in the lives of your church families? Which of these needs will a camp help to satisfy? What do you hope to accomplish in the lives of the families who attend? Be sure you state your goals in terms of what the family (rather than the staff) will accomplish. For example, one goal might be, "Parents will practice listening to their children's statements and restating them in order to be sure they have understood." (Not, "We will teach parents to listen to their children.") Use these basic goals and interest-finder results (described later) to guide your decisions in developing the camp program.

The director's first act should be to contact the denominational camping coordinator for information regarding the denomination's campsite. If the denomination does not have this kind of facility, contact Christian Camping International (P.O. Box 400, Somonauk, IL 60552) or the American Camping Association (Bradford Woods, Martinsville, IN 46151). In some areas you may have to reserve camp facilities as much as a year in advance.

Look for a conference center that provides adequate housing for families, either in single or duplex cabins or in dormitories that can be divided into small areas. Find a location that is no more than two or three hours' drive (or half a tank of gas) from your church. Preferably, choose a camp facility that has a resident cook, lifeguard and other service personnel. Often you can supplement this staff with your own counselors, kitchen assistants, recreation leaders, speakers, and so on.

A small church without enough people to fill a conference center might consider some options. One possibility is to link up with one or more churches in the local area, or with other churches in the denomination, and have a multi-church family camp at a facility that is conveniently located for all participating congregations. Another idea is for interested families to get together at a state or national park. Families can cook their own meals or take turns cooking for the group. Pastor and parents can work together to plan Bible study, campfire sing-times, hikes and other activities.

Choose your camp dates with other church, school, and community activities in mind: Does your school district offer summer school for children? When are your age-graded youth camps and vacation Bible school? Will such occurrences as a special harvest period or a vacation shut-down of a major local industry affect your choice of dates?

Before determining the program for family camp, circulate among the families of your church and/or community an interest finder so your camp program will "scratch where people itch." Include in your interest finder such items as:

"Family camp is an opportunity to . . ."

"Family camp means we can . . ."

"The thing I like best about our family is . . ."

"Our family wants family camp to be . . ."

"The subjects our family needs to discuss are . . ."

With the results in mind, plan speakers and learning activities to help families meet some of the needs they've expressed on the interest finder.

If you plan to have one or more featured speakers, communicate with them as early as possible and confirm all arrangements: dates, remuneration, nature of responsibilities, theme of camp, nature of audience. Be sure speaker(s) make *definite plans* to involve campers in small-group discussions, problem-solving, and other two-way activities in order to avoid a "sit still and listen" type of program.

Recruit from your church several other staff members, including:

Child-care personnel for children under four years during day and for children who go to bed early at night.

Assistant camp directors to plan and supervise age-graded programs for children and youth.

    a. A counselor and assistant for every eight to ten children who are age four through second grade.

    b. A counselor and assistant for every ten to twelve middlers, juniors and youth.

One or more *craft leaders*. (See section on "Resources" for craft project sources.)

A supply coordinator. Plan to check out and in on a daily basis all craft supplies and recreation equipment.

Several young people, high school age and older, to help with recreational activities.

A leader for the evening campfire program.

A lifeguard and *first-aid specialist;* a *nature leader* who is knowledgeable about the natural features of the site (unless the conference center offers these services).

Kitchen helpers, if the conference center requires that you help with this work. You might recruit young people and pay them, or pass the KP duty around among the families who attend.

A registrar to handle registration fees, room or cabin assignments.

A publicity coordinator. Publicity for family camp must begin early. Give the dates, cost, place and name of the special speaker. Aim publicity primarily at church members. (See chapter on "Publicizing Your Program" for detailed suggestions.)

A transportation coordinator to arrange car pools or a bus for those who prefer bus transportation. Also, provide a travel pack for each family (lists of things to bring, conference program, map to camp grounds, games to play en route).

Read the chapter on "Training Your Staff" for helpful ideas in training your volunteer staff members. Include a trip to the campsite in the training schedule. Tour the grounds, meet with the camp administrator to discuss facilities and programming. Actually go through a typical day's schedule as you have planned it.

Perhaps your conference center provides help in training your staff and suggesting program details. Some camps have printed materials; others even provide a staff member to help train counselors at the churches that use their conference facilities.

Take advantage of all the opportunities offered by the conference center. These might include horse-drawn hayrides, horseback riding, ball games, croquet, shuffleboard, archery, hiking, swimming, boating, crafts and projects, indoor games.

Plan family craft projects for each family to take home. For example, a large burlap banner for the family to decorate with felt and yarn; or a fabric place mat for each family member to decorate with felt pens and liquid embroidery. Suggest that the decoration ideas reflect your conference theme. If your program theme is "Ways to Please Jesus," campers might draw reminders of things they might do to please Jesus (a toy to represent sharing, a dollar sign to represent giving, a smiling face to represent a cheerful attitude).

The effectiveness of your family camp will depend in large measure upon the kind of daily program you develop. A few of the children's and youth activities will be separate from those for adults. However, remember that your primary purpose is to unite families, not to separate them. Plan your schedule to achieve each of the goals you want to accomplish.

Adapt the following general schedule to meet your particular needs. The times indicated are suggestions only. Set your own time schedule in consultation with your assistant directors and the camp staff.

FRIDAY NIGHT (of a weekend camp)

7:00 P.M.—Arrival, room assignments, unpacking, indoor games.

8:00 P.M.—Refreshments (cocoa, coffee, tea, milk, punch, fruit, cookies, cheese, vegetable sticks, crackers are possibilities).

8:30 A.M.—Small children to bed (child care provided).

8:45 P.M.—Junior and senior highs have discussion, speaker, or film, and recreation. Adults have first session with speaker or Bible study material.

SATURDAY (of weekend camp) or
EACH DAY (of week-long camp)

7:00 A.M.—Rise n' shine!

8:00 A.M.—Breakfast (families eat together).

8:45 A.M.—Family devotions (individual families or all families together).

9:15 A.M.—Parents: Bible study and small group discussion (coffee or tea). Children: Age-graded Bible study. (Child care for those under four.)

11:00 A.M.—Parents: Elective seminars (topics from family interest finders). Children: Game time/recreation.

12:30 P.M.—Lunch (families eat together).

1:30 P.M.—Family activities and recreation. Options, such as: horse-drawn hayrides, horseback riding, ball games, croquet, shuffleboard, hiking, crafts and projects, indoor games. (Child care provided for little ones who need naps.)

5:30 P.M.—Dinner (families eat together).

7:00 P.M.—Vesper time (separate children's sessions).

7:30 P.M.—Family campfire.

8:30 P.M.—Children to bed. Youth and adults meet for film and discussion.

SUNDAY (of weekend camp)

8:00 A.M.—Breakfast (families eat together).

8:45 A.M.—Family devotions (individual families or all families together).

9:15 A.M.—Parents: Bible study and small-group discussion (coffee).

Children: Age-graded Bible study (optional: include planning for participating in worship). (Child care for those under four).

10:45 A.M.—Worship (families together).

12:00 P.M.—Lunch (families eat together).

2:00 P.M.—Camp closes.

Plan your staff meeting after lunch (when families relax together) each day of a week-long camp, or on Saturday noon of a weekend camp. Provide ample opportunity for each staff member to share blessings and problems. Pray. Then work together to solve problems. Keep staff meeting to thirty minutes so staff members don't miss out on needed rest or recreation. If a child-care center is functioning during this time, provide another opportunity for those staff members to meet with camp leaders to share and pray.

Keep the program relaxed and easy-going by allowing plenty of time for each kind of activity. Don't let the evening sessions run late. Remember that younger children get sleepy quite early. If child care is provided, let younger children go to bed while older children, youth and adults have additional family activities.

Provide a separate child-care center for babies where parents may pick up their little ones for all meals and for any other time they may choose. Be sure children in the care center during the afternoon have opportunity for a nap. During the rest of the day keep them occupied with stories, short walks around the grounds, and other appropriate kinds of activities (see section "Resources" for activity resources).

You can easily adapt VBS Bible curriculum to the morning Bible study times for the various ages. Most VBS curricula offer complete Bible teaching programs for each age level. VBS courses include age level teacher's manual, students' materials, correlated teaching resources and creative craft projects.

Christian family-oriented magazines, such as *Family Life Today* offer a variety of resources for family devotions, projects and activities appropriate to a family camp. Provide a copy of this kind of material for each family. Another excellent resource is *Adventure Through the Bible*, a four-page take-home paper with Bible stories and suggestions for family-time activities. (See chapter entitled "Resources.")

Chapter 6

Intergenerational Programs

Traditionally, church programs separate people by age—children here, youth there, adults in yet another location. However, there is a growing trend to bring together people of various ages, especially with a view to strengthening family ties. This trend involves what is called intergenerational study.

Intergenerational programs bring together people of different generations. The various age groups study the same material and live the same experiences during the learning session. In some cases, all-together-times alternate with brief times of separate study for children and adults. Even so, the different age groups work on similar or parallel material, and when they come together again they share from a common basis.

Although such programs can help build family relationships, they do not exclude singles, couples without children, older people, or children and young people who attend without their parents. Groupings in an intergenerational study are flexible enough to sustain the interest of each person and let each one benefit from the special insights of the others. In addition, this sort of study can permit most of the program's staff people to participate with their own families in the study activities.

A summer Bible ministry with an intergenerational approach would work well as an evening program (similar to evening VBS except for keeping the age groups together). Such a program might be held nightly for a week or two, or once a week for several weeks. For example, G/L's *Family Values Workshop* is a five-session intergenerational study. You may want to schedule this workshop for an intensive week of nightly meetings or spread it over five weeks. In determining your schedule, consider factors suggested in the chapters on "VBS" and "Evening VBS."

Your planning, recruiting and training will need to cover the same bases as for VBS; see chapters on "VBS," "Recruiting Your Staff" and "Training Your Staff." See contents for "Bible Ministries Countdown Schedule."

Your staff may need extra encouragement if they are unfamiliar with guiding people of differing ages in studying together. Keep an enthusiastic attitude and others will "catch" it. Churches that have tried the intergenerational approach have found it worth the effort.

For curriculum, consider the *Family Values Workshop;* or use ideas from G/L's *Adventure Through the Bible* take-home papers, which have a Bible study plus family and kids-only activity suggestions. (See "Resources" for other material.)

en. Such a program might be held nigh
for several weeks. For example, G

Chapter 7

Additional Ministries

So far we have suggested for your consideration several Bible ministries—VBS, day camp, family camp and so on. This chapter is the place where you can take off in a leap of imagination. Here are a number of ideas for ministries; it's up to you to imagine how one or more of them can help accomplish goals within the priorities of your church. Remember to do the same kind of careful planning any ministry deserves!

HOLIDAY VBS

How about a mini-VBS-type ministry during the Christmas or Easter season? For Bible study materials, use the seasonally-oriented units from your church school curriculum. Or have a snow camp where sledding and ski facilities are available. Use VBS Bible study plans for school age children and/or youth; family camp plans for entire families.

Some churches send witness teams to popular beach and vacation resorts during the Easter holidays to share Christ with vacationing students. Perhaps your church would encourage and support your young people in a similar ministry. This kind of ministry requires careful planning and training, and an experienced adult staff.

CHOIR TOUR

A young people's choir might work out a tour schedule. Begin with weekend trips. Then work up to longer tours during vacation periods. The choir shares a well-thought-out and well-rehearsed package of music with people who don't have many opportunities to hear live good music.

Choir tours often visit other churches—but how about considering nursing homes, convalescent homes, retirement centers, orphanages, schools for mentally or physically handicapped children, or even prisons where satisfactory arrangements can be made?

A choir tour requires much careful planning. You must provide transportation, arrange for housing and meals on the road, and prepare the young people to consider the trip a ministry, not just a vacation. (See "Outreach" section that follows for suggestions.)

Even without traveling away from home, young people could prepare a program to present to local nursing homes, rescue missions, and other institutions as suggested above—including the local jail.

Young people can give parties at children's homes, retirement homes, or low-income housing centers. This kind of ministry takes careful preparation, adult supervision, and proper arrangements with the people in charge of the selected institutions.

OUTREACH

Some churches program youth outreach to inner city or rural churches, Indian schools or reservations, migrant camps, and people across the Mexican border.

Young people and vacationing adults can spend a week with an inner city or rural church—painting, scrubbing, making repairs—and thus share Christ's love with their Christian brothers and sisters. Close the week with a potluck dinner party, with choirs or other special talent from both churches.

Another form of outreach to an inner city or rural church is to recycle your VBS. Reuse the time and effort your staff spent in planning and training by sharing with a church that would not otherwise be able to have a summer program. Get the names of one or more such churches and offer the services and experience of your staff of young people and adults. The cost of such an outreach is minimal, requiring only the replacement of student books and craft supplies.

Young people visiting Indian or Mexican sites during Easter or summer vacation can help build buildings, clean up existing ones, teach the host young people, learn their customs and lore, and share Christ's love.

Here are pointers to help you plan your youth outreach:

1. *Begin planning early,* at least four to six months before your depar-

ture. It takes time to confirm a place to minister, develop a training program, arrange for enroute lodging, meals and bathing facilities, and the many other details that are a part of a travel camp.

2. *Develop the itinerary,* considering five key factors:

First, choose a place to minister. Contact your regional or denominational offices or other Christian service agency for leads. Select a site that is within reasonable driving time so that you don't spend the entire week traveling. Be sure your group's abilities mesh with the needs of those whom you will serve.

Second, arrange for enroute camping sites or other lodging. Bathing and toilet facilities are particularly important, especially if yours is a co-ed group. If you're camping out, check with campgrounds ahead of time to be sure they can accommodate a group your size. To be sure of accommodations, make reservations for campsites in advance.

Third, include some spots of scenic beauty for a quiet Bible-study setting to point your young people to God, the Creator and loving Father.

Fourth, plan occasional recreational stops along the way. Hours of riding in a bus or car can produce lots of pent-up youthful energy that needs an acceptable outlet. Hiking, swimming, volleyball and other kinds of physical activities can avoid many problems.

Fifth, plan your overnight stops within easy driving distance of each other, probably no more than 400 miles. Federal regulations require that interstate bus drivers have an eight-hour break after ten hours of driving. (While drivers of church-owned buses are exempt, in some *states,* it is a worthwhile rule to follow for the safety of all.)

3. *Recruit your staff.* You will need adult sponsors, a bus driver (unless you charter a bus), cooks and a nurse or someone well trained in first aid. (This person may also be one of the sponsors or cooks, or the driver.) The cooks play a strategic role in a travel camp. It isn't easy to cook for a large group of people, particularly in a camping situation. Be sure the cooks understand the limitations of the kitchen facilities and plan their menus accordingly. Consider using a recreational vehicle for a "chuck wagon."

4. *Determine costs.* Food will be a major expense. Plan the costs of each meal to arrive at a daily per person cost. Other costs to consider are transportation (include the cost of gasoline in your calculations, or the cost of chartering a bus if that is your plan) and spending money the campers will want for souvenirs.

5. *Develop a training program.* Establish standards both for attendance at the training sessions and for behavior on the trip. Require

attendance at a percentage of the training schedule you develop—such as four out of five sessions.

Standards of behavior should be discussed at the training sessions. Couples who are dating should definitely understand that they will be expected to avoid all display of amorous feelings on this trip. Different cultures misinterpret these displays of affection. Such misunderstanding could ruin your entire ministry.

Campers also should understand that they will be sharing responsibility for setting up and breaking camp, KP duty, and packing the bus. If you pack sack lunches each night (so that you won't have to stop and wait for the cooks to prepare lunch), the campers should know that some of them will be asked to help the cooks prepare and pack the lunches.

Include some orientation regarding the people and culture to whom your campers will minister; make sure they understand that other people's customs may be different, but that does not make them inferior as a people or a society. Warn young people against developing an arrogant or critical attitude toward other people's customs and culture.

Your training sessions will also include rehearsals and help for the young people in developing their ministries. Each one should know how to *Give an answer to everyone who asks you to give the reason for the hope that you have* (1 Pet. 3:15).

6. *Have the campers' parents sign a medical release form* (see contents for sample form) granting permission to the travel camp leader to get any medical attention needed by the camper. Let parents know what sort of medical or first-aid care will be available while traveling and at the destination.

7. *Develop checklists and a packing plan.* The equipment needed for a travel camp can easily be lost or forgotten. A checklist on a clipboard will help you take a quick inventory.

Carefully think through a packing plan. The things you will need first should be packed last.

It is helpful to assign a number to each camper. Have campers "count off" when returning to the bus. This procedure can prevent the embarrassment and distress of driving off and leaving a camper in a restroom.

8. *Plan to report the results* of your travel mission camp to your home church. A special youth night service can help the whole church feel it was a part of their young people's ministry. Slides and testimonies by the campers can make the venture a highlight for the entire church.

the training schedule you develop—such

Part III

How To Plan and Organize Your Ministry

"If you don't know where you're going, any road will get you there," a familiar quotation suggests. To effectively guide children, youth or adults into a consciousness of God's love and care, leaders and teachers MUST know where they're going. And "any road" simply won't do! So that the entire staff of your Bible ministry can determine the ways they will communicate scriptural truths in a Bible ministry setting, you need to make planning and preparation your next consideration.

Carefully read and think about the following steps. Pray as you read, asking God to give you wisdom and insight for your task.

Chapter 8

Recruiting Your Staff

BEGIN EARLY

Recruiting can be one of the most rewarding aspects of your Bible program if it is done as a result of careful, thoughtful, prayerful planning.

Start with prayer, asking the Father to direct your recruiting efforts and to begin preparing the people He wants involved in your ministry.

Then review some recruiting resources. Two helpful items are the ICL booklet *Recruit . . . Train . . . Plan* and the ICL filmstrip *Recruiting Is Everybody's Job.* (See "Resources" section for further information.)

Develop a procedures manual for the director of the ministry you have chosen. Include in it step-by-step details of planning and carrying out the ministry. (You can use the information in this book regarding your particular ministry, adapting it to the specifics of your facilities, program and staff.)

List the personnel needs for your Bible ministry. Then write a "job description" for each position. Include the planning and preparation requirements, and meetings to be attended, as well as the duties during the Bible ministry. Knowing exactly what is expected will help a person make an intelligent decision about accepting the position, and then will help the recruited staff person to do the best possible job. Sample job descriptions are found in this chapter.

As you develop your job descriptions, consider the possibility of having more than one person involved in the key positions. For example, one church asks for a two-year commitment for the job of director. The first year, the new volunteer is co-director, working with and learning from the director. Next year, the former co-director is the director, training a new recruit.

FOLLOW A PLAN

Prepare a countdown schedule. After you have chosen your department leaders, meet with them to discuss a staff recruitment schedule. The "Bible Ministries Countdown Schedule" (at the end of Part I) will help.

About sixteen weeks before your Bible ministry begins, announce the dates and times in your church bulletin and newsletter. Include in your announcement information about when and where volunteers can sign up—"Do it early so you can have your choice of a place to serve."

About three months before your Bible ministry, prepare a flyer to insert in your church bulletin for two Sundays, requesting volunteer help for your Bible ministry. Members may place completed flyers in offering plates. Telephone those who respond and tell them of the various positions open in the area of interest they checked. A sample flyer is shown on page 58. (The reverse side may be decorated with art depicting the theme of your Bible ministry.)

Another recruiting method that is used successfully by the Evangelical Free church in Fullerton, California is a Vacation Bible School Potluck Luncheon. It is held in May at the church fellowship hall. Attendees bring salads. Child care is provided (children bring their own sack lunches). People are encouraged to attend the luncheon if they are interested in helping with Bible school, or even if they are unable to be involved but want to help recruit others by "bringing a buddy" to the luncheon. Music, skits, and a preview of the VBS material make for a lively program.

Another possibility is a prayerfully planned Sunday service in which congregational singing, special music, Scripture and the message all promote the value of the Bible ministry and the joy of involvement. Descriptions of staff positions available and the duties involved will help people understand how they can become "fellow workers" with the Lord in ministering to the students.

One church publishes a newsletter for their Bible school. Beginning in May, the letter provides both publicity and recruiting helps. "Want Ads," for example, were used in one issue to describe various staff positions for which volunteers were needed.

During (date), our church will be helping children and youth learn of the Lord Jesus. You can be a part of this exciting Bible ministry.

Complete the information indicating where you feel God would have you serve. Then give this flyer to one of the ushers or place it in the offering plate or take it to the church office. You'll be contacted regarding the important part you can have in our Bible ministry.

(THE NAME OF YOUR BIBLE MINISTRY)

YES! I'm willing to help with the following age group:

Ages:	2 & 3	_____
	4 & 5	_____
Grades:	1 & 2	_____
	3 & 4	_____
	5 & 6	_____
	7 & 8	_____

I will serve as:
- class teacher _____
- assistant _____
- pianist _____
- craft leader/helper _____
- secretary _____
- recreation leader _____
- refreshment coordinator/helper _____
- wherever needed _____
(List other positions you have open.)

Name _____

Address _____

Phone _____

Can we reach you by phone in the _____ morning _____ afternoon _____ evening.

Recruit prayer partners right along with staff members. Ask that people who are unable to participate actively in your Bible ministry sign up to pray. Match prayer partners with staff people for a personal relationship and specific prayer requests.

Once you have begun your general appeals for staff, you can begin to focus on individuals. Be careful to talk to each person who completes an information card. Help him/her to determine the position for greatest effectiveness. In addition, you may want to recruit others who have not filled out cards, but who you feel may be willing and able to serve. In either case, follow these steps for recruiting individuals:

1. Present the opportunity for service in a manner that is in accord with the importance of that service. In other words, don't just telephone or buttonhole people when you see them at church. Instead, make an appointment to visit the person at home.

2. Take along materials pertaining to the job. If you have literature describing the curriculum—or the curriculum itself—take that. Assure the prospect that you will supply all the essentials needed to fulfill the responsibility which you are asking him or her to accept.

3. Briefly discuss the purpose of the Bible ministry and the position you want the person to consider. Explain how that position will contribute to fulfilling the goals of the ministry. Be enthusiastic!

4. Explain the duties of the position. Bring a job description and go over it in detail. Give an estimate of the amount of time that the position will require, from advance training through the final wrap-up after the ministry is concluded.

5. Explain the support systems provided for staff people. For example, some churches assure teachers of a class ratio of no more than eight students per teacher. Thus a teacher understands that the class will be manageable. Another vital support system is specific and thorough training for the position, so that the staff person will be prepared and will feel adequate. Mothers will need child care for their little ones who are too young to be enrolled in the Bible ministry. Some churches provide lunch for all staff members each day of the Bible ministry. Others arrange car pools so that people without transportation can be involved.

6. Ask the recruit to pray earnestly and to let the Holy Spirit guide in reaching a decision. You do not want a decision now, but only after prayer.

7. Return after an agreed-upon time or indicate when you will call the person to receive the decision.

8. If the decision is negative, encourage the person to consider working in other areas of the ministry that may better suit his or her abilities, interests and gifts. If the answer is yes, assure your new staff person of continuing support; work closely with the recruit as he or she prepares and serves.

Following are job descriptions for staff members of Bible ministries:

DIRECTOR

As director, you are responsible for several areas of work:

1. Overall planning of your Bible ministry. Carefully read this entire book and the procedures manual provided by your church. Begin planning as early as possible and set up a step-by-step schedule to guide you in your preparation. (See Part V for "Bible Ministries Countdown Schedule.")

2. Staff recruitment. Start by recruiting your key co-director (who will make a commitment to be director next year working with the new co-director), key leaders—the department leaders and special program coordinators (publicity, crafts, missions, recreation, and so on); then have these key people help you list names of potential staff members. Look for the basic qualities needed—spiritual concern, willingness to learn, ability to work with others, enthusiasm and capability. Then begin the recruiting procedures suggested earlier in this chapter.

Use these ratios for department staff: prekindergarten—one teacher for every four to five students; kindergarten—one for every five to six students; primary, middler and junior—one for each seven to eight students; youth—one for every eight to ten students.

Consider all possible sources for your staff: church members, last year's summer staff, college and seminary students, teenagers, church school substitute teachers, public school teachers, retired men and women.

3. Staff training. See "Training Your Staff." Go over this plan in detail with your co-director and department leaders, adapting it as necessary to fit your specific situation.

Be alert to other training opportunities, such as denomination or G/L Publications' VBS presentations or clinics in your area, ICL seminars and clinics (your church supplier has this information), your own training courses, material from the church library, observation of other Bible ministries, private conferences.

4. Facility selection and assignment. If you are conducting a VBS, you will probably meet in your church facilities. With your department leaders, decide how best to use your facilities for the school. If possible, have each department meet in the same area used in Sunday School so that the children will feel at home. (See descriptions of the various ministries for further information on facility selection.)

If your Bible ministry includes an away-from-church program (such as day camp, family camp, backyard Bible clubs), you will probably be responsible to select these sites. Determine a location as early as possible, for much of your planning and work depends upon this decision. (See descriptions of the ministries for further information on facility selection.) Involve your key leaders in deciding the best way to use the site or facilities you choose.

5. Scheduling. General scheduling of the program is your responsibility. Your departmental leaders can help, but the final decisions that will avoid conflicts in facility use are yours. Outline your daily schedule in detail, check it with your co-director and department leaders, then duplicate it for everyone.

Meet with your co-director, coordinators and department leaders as often as is necessary to plan your Bible ministry. Give each of these staff members authority to follow through in her or his area of work, without having to check with you about every detail. Make yourself available to them however, for any problem that requires your involvement.

CO-DIRECTOR

You are learning the job of director in preparation for being next year's director. Work closely with the director, attending all meetings and conferences. Perform tasks assigned to you by director. See "Director" job description for an idea of what is involved in this ministry.

DEPARTMENT LEADER

You are responsible for the smooth functioning of your department. Your planning and supervising may include all or some of the following duties.

Before the Bible Ministry

1. Meet with the director to determine staff, schedule, needed materials, including curriculum materials for your department.

2. If you have never worked as a department leader before, attend the three training meetings for department leaders on _____, _____, and _____ (dates).

3. Meet with people responsible for crafts, missions, supplies and refreshments. Make specific plans for their duties in your department.

4. Recruit the staff by _____ (date). You will need _____ teachers (specify number needed); _____ helpers. Provide a list of your staff to _____ (name of director) by _____ (date).

5. Attend four training meetings on _____ (dates and times). You will spend at least part of each meeting with your departmental staff,

helping them to prepare for their responsibilities in the Bible ministry.

6. Give specific assignments to each teacher and other staff member in the department.

7. Discuss with your staff procedures concerning discipline, refreshments, moving from one activity to another, and so on.

8. Determine all materials needed for your department; obtain them from the supply coordinator.

9. See that all necessary equipment is in the department.

10. Work with the pianist or other accompanist to learn all songs you will use during your Bible ministry.

11. Pray for your staff before and during the Bible ministry.

During the Bible Ministry

1. Supervise (not lead) all departmental activities and keep department on schedule.

2. Conduct worship time.

3. Obtain additional needed supplies.

4. See that all student records are complete.

5. Encourage staff and praise good work done by staff and students.

6. Maintain communication between the ministry director and department staff.

7. Obtain suitable substitutes for absent teachers or other staff.

8. Conduct staff meetings as needed either before or after each session of the Bible ministry.

9. Complete the plans for your department's part in the closing program and supervise preparation of the department for the program.

10. Handle any emergencies pertaining to the department or students.

After the Bible Ministry

1. Thank each teacher and other staff member personally.

2. See that all supplies and curriculum materials are counted and returned to the proper people.

3. Write an evaluation of the department's activities, noting strengths, weaknesses and suggestions for next year. Give evaluation to director.

4. Follow up new students in cooperation with Sunday School personnel.

5. Take down all decorations and remove all equipment that should not remain in the room.

REGISTRAR/SECRETARY

Good records are essential for evaluation and planning next year. Complete information is also essential for proper follow-up. You are responsible for the following tasks.

1. Help with (or be in charge of) preregistration. Be sure registration cards are completely filled out. Cards are available from your church supplier.

2. Sort preregistration cards and give to department leaders and other appropriate leaders.

3. Be sure lists of staff are complete with addresses and phone numbers. Keep this list up to date at all times.

4. Keep records of daily attendance and offerings as they are given to you by the departments.

5. Prepare and distribute any memos to personnel from the director. Post copies of the memos in a conspicuous place for permanent reference.

6. Prepare any special notices that the children are to take home— such as announcements regarding missionary project, offering, closing program.

7. Duplicate materials for department leaders as directed.

8. Prepare final report, listing total and average attendance by departments, decisions, offering, etc.

MISSIONS COORDINATOR

As the missions coordinator you provide an opportunity for believers to share the gospel with others.

The aim of the missionary program is fourfold:

1. Educate students concerning the missions work now being supported by the church and those doing the work.

2. Encourage students to pray specifically for missionary needs.

3. Provide opportunity for students to give to a missionary project.

4. Challenge each person to consider the Great Commission in relation to his or her own life.

What can the missionary coordinator do to fulfill these aims?

1. Decide on a missionary project. If your church does not have a missionary or project to suggest, contact your denominational missions headquarters or an independent missions agency.

2. Contact a missionary (well in advance) to speak about your chosen project. Be sure the missionary understands the age level of his or her

audience and is informed about the project. If appropriate, have the missionary dress in the native costume of the people with whom she or he works. The children of missionaries may also tell about life on the mission field from their point of view.

3. Investigate the availability of filmstrips, films, slides, and other visual aids. Order well in advance.

4. Secure books and other literature for reference. Have books on missions and missionaries available for students to take home and read. Perhaps a group in the church could add some missionary books to the church library.

5. Set up an attractive display of curios which the students may handle. Arrange a bulletin board with maps and pictures to stimulate interest. Help with departmental displays.

6. Plan the presentation of the chosen project with each department leader. Provide any literature needed by teachers.

7. Plan a visual record (such as a chart or poster) to show the giving of each department or the entire school. (Try a little creativity! One church decided that the VBS offering would be used to purchase a motorcycle needed by a missionary. They borrowed a motorcycle from a dealer. The first day of VBS they let the students examine it, and they explained the purpose of the missionary offering. Then they covered the cycle with a sheet. Each subsequent day, they uncovered the portion of the motorcycle that had been "paid for" by that day's offering.)

SUPPLY COORDINATOR

A central clearinghouse for supply purchasing and distribution is important for economical and efficient operation of each Bible ministry. Your tasks include:

1. Based on last year's attendance lists and knowledge of any foreseen changes, order teachers' and students' books, teaching resources and craft kits.

2. Each department may need items such as paper fasteners, yarn, paste and colored construction paper. You can save money if you buy the supplies all at once and in bulk. Have each department leader figure anticipated needs and turn in a list of needed supplies two weeks before your Bible ministry begins. You will purchase, divide, and distribute these supplies. Check for discounts available to church groups.

3. Work with the finance coordinator regarding the method of paying for items.

4. Collect crayons and scissors from each Sunday School department (keep track of how many from where) and distribute where needed in the program.

5. Secure additional supplies as needed during your Bible ministry.

6. Receive all unused books and leftover supplies at the close of the program. Make an itemized list of supplies that can be used next year or the year after. Store reusable material. Return borrowed equipment!

7. Turn in all records to the director to be filed for reference next year.

CRAFT COORDINATOR

Here are some ways you can help make craft time worthwhile as well as fun:

1. Work with the director to select which of the recommended craft kits you will use for each age group. Or plan other projects, such as those suggested in the teacher's manual for each department. Make up a sample of each project you choose.

2. Submit a list of needed materials to the supply coordinator two or three months before your Bible ministry begins. If you gather your own materials, begin advertising for them several months in advance. Ask church members to bring such items as foil pie tins, tubes from waxed paper or paper towel rolls, scraps of yarn and cloth, or whatever is needed for your projects.

3. Prepare clear, exact directions for volunteers who will be helping you prepare the crafts. Give volunteers a correctly completed example of each craft project.

4. Each day during the program see that supplies are laid out, then carefully put away after the craft period.

5. Arrange a place to keep unfinished projects. Be sure all students put their names on their projects.

6. When the program is over, return unused supplies to the supply coordinator.

7. Make a written summary and evaluation of the craft program for the director.

8. Return all unclaimed but finished crafts made by the children to department leaders to be used in follow-up.

REFRESHMENT COORDINATOR

Refreshments are a welcome treat for every age group. Some churches furnish milk or punch and cookies (often donated by church members).

Others, as expenses and donations make it possible, provide more varied refreshments, including fruit juice, cheese and crackers, vegetable sticks, and fresh fruit.

1. Purchase punch concentrate, juice, or milk and paper cups to meet estimated needs for the entire program. (If your program will last longer than a week, purchase milk for one week at a time.)

2. Through the church bulletin and women's organizations, ask for donations of the refreshments you plan to provide. Be very clear about exactly what kind of food you want and how much of each item. (For example, ten dozen cookies; no chocolate chip or other chocolate types, since many people have problems with chocolate. Or, five paper plates full of celery stuffed with peanut butter.) Specify the kind of container in which the food should be brought (plastic bags, paper plates, clean coffee cans with lids). Arrange and announce a central place to leave donated refreshments. (You can freeze cookies for several weeks before the program begins, but vegetables and fruit should be brought almost daily.)

3. Each day check to see if there are enough refreshments for the next day. If more are needed, call people and ask for more, or purchase them. If using cookies, check bulk prices at your local market or day-old bakery outlet. Many stores give discounts to churches.

4. Be sure there are enough pitchers and other equipment to prepare and serve the refreshments.

5. Supervise the distribution of the refreshments to each group. Be sure the department leader has someone lead the children in thanks to God for the food.

6. Turn in an evaluation and a financial report to your director, with suggestions for next year's program.

TRANSPORTATION COORDINATOR

Very few church programs draw only boys and girls from within walking distance of the church or other facility being used. It is your job to see that as many as possible are transported to your Bible ministry.

1. If your church has a bus, decide if it will be sufficient. If not, rent or borrow additional buses, or arrange for cars and drivers.

2. Check insurance on your bus to be certain your Bible ministry is covered. Also check coverage on borrowed or rented buses.

3. Secure drivers for buses. Check your insurance policy for driver requirements. List all drivers with your insurance company.

4. If a bus or buses are to be used, map out routes and time schedules.

See that the schedules are duplicated and distributed in Sunday School and church, at the pre-summer rally, and other appropriate times and places. To determine the route, check the regular route of your Sunday School bus and preregistration cards for the location of children. Perhaps there are housing areas and other key locations you should plan to reach for your Bible ministry.

5. Keep careful records of expenditures so the bills can be paid from the Bible ministry budget.

6. Arrange for someone to ride on each bus in addition to the driver to help children in and out of the bus, act as street guard, maintain order and make sure everyone is on the bus when it is time to go home.

7. If cars are used, act as a clearinghouse for information regarding drivers who have extra room. Advertise the pick-up service with a telephone number to call.

8. If teachers and other staff members need transportation, arrange car pools for them.

FINANCE COORDINATOR

Careful use of God's money is the primary responsibility of the finance coordinator. It's your job to see that your Bible ministry is adequately financed, and that the money allocated for the program is wisely spent. To fulfill these responsibilities you will:

1. Work with your church treasurer or other responsible individual or group to decide how much money will be made available by the church for your program.

2. Prepare a detailed budget for the program, working with the other coordinators, department leaders and general director.

3. Devise ways to secure additional funds necessary to underwrite expenses (see suggestions that follow).

4. If your Bible ministry involves a student fee, work with the registrar/secretary to devise a system for collecting this fee from each student.

5. Develop a requisition system to control expenses. Do not allow anyone to spend any money without a previously authorized requisition.

6. Maintain complete and accurate records of all expenses (with requisitions and receipts), and all income (with date and source).

7. See that all bills are paid promptly. If bills are to be paid through the church treasurer, clear your plans for payment with him or her.

8. At the end of your program prepare a complete, detailed financial report and turn it in to your director.

Here are some ways to raise money for your Bible ministry:

1. Ask the church to designate all or a major part of the money from the church budget.

2. Take special offerings at church services before your program begins. Be sure you clear this plan with your church treasurer to avoid any feeling that you are diverting gifts from the church's regular budget.

3. Take an offering at the closing program. If this is necessary, present the need in such a way that the parents will not feel that "The church is always begging for money." Let them know just how much the program costs per student; give them an opportunity to help cover that cost without "high pressuring" them.

4. Send an offering envelope home with each student three days before the program ends, with a note inviting parents to contribute to the cost. Tell them that all money received in the envelopes will go to underwrite the program's costs.

5. Charge each student a minimum fee, varying with the length and elaborateness of the program. A two-week day camp, for example, will certainly entail an appropriate student fee. On the other hand, a one-week VBS or backyard Bible school might not require this source of income.

6. Invite church members to donate "scholarships" for students who cannot pay their own way.

7. Invite an adult Sunday School class to sponsor a child (or several children).

8. Plan for the children to purchase their own craft kits or materials. You'll need to state this information clearly in all publicity.

9. Plan fund-raising activities. Perhaps the young people can stage a paper drive, car wash, or bake sale, or auction themselves off as "servants for a day" to do housework and yardwork in exchange for donations to the Bible ministry. Sponsor a "10-kilometer" or other length of walk or run, with modest entrance fees going to the ministry fund. Let people get their heads together and they will come up with many fund-raising ideas.

PUBLICITY COORDINATOR

Your primary responsibilities are to recruit students from the church and community, and to help the director recruit staff members from the church membership. To achieve these objectives you will:

1. Plan, in cooperation with your director and co-director, a comprehensive publicity campaign. "Publicizing Your Program" suggests a general plan for this campaign.

2. Devise a schedule for the preparation and implementation of each kind of publicity you have included in your campaign.

3. Prepare a detailed budget, and control expenditures so they do not exceed that budget.

4. Recruit assistants to help you—poster makers, visitors, people to conduct the neighborhood canvass, coordinators of the pre-summer rally and VBS parade, and so on.

5. Supervise the implementation of each step in your campaign.

6. Evaluate the effectiveness of each kind of promotion, and submit a written report on your work to the director at the end of the program.

In addition to recruiting students, you will work with the director and co-director to publicize staff needs and to recruit workers. The recruiting suggestions at the beginning of this chapter indicate several ways you can help your director in this vital work.

TEACHER

You are on the front lines of the Bible ministry. You will:

1. Attend training meetings and planning meetings scheduled for your department. (Include dates and times.)

2. Be present every day of the Bible ministry _____ (dates), arriving no later than _____ (time).

3. Prayerfully prepare the lessons. Learn the memory verses you will be assigning to your pupils. Make sure you understand how every segment of the daily program helps accomplish the Bible teaching/learning aims and where your responsibilities lie.

4. Present the Bible study to your pupils. Lead in the workbook, memory work, crafts, refreshments, or other areas assigned by your department leader.

5. Be prepared to lead children to Christ (see chapter on "Leading a Child to Christ").

OTHER STAFF POSITIONS

Depending upon the ministry you have chosen, you may need additional staff people. The chapters describing the various ministries provide further information on the tasks involved in each position. Additional staff may include: lifeguard; first aid person or nurse; nature guide, food crew members or cooks; counselors, assistant counselors; bus driver(s); bus chaperon; hostess; child care personnel; recreation leaders; campfire leader.

Chapter 9

Training Your Staff

Training is absolutely vital to the success of the Bible ministry you have selected. The better prepared the staff is, the more effective the program will be. Your staff people are volunteers who have high expectations. They want to succeed, and a thorough training program will help them to do so.

The whole idea of a Bible ministry is to serve God and to minister to others in His name. Our Lord wants the best from each of us. He expects church leaders *to prepare God's people for works of service, so that the body of Christ may be built up (Eph. 4:12)*. Training your staff is one way to prepare them for their *works of service*.

Your training program serves another purpose. As your people prepare together for their ministry, they develop a team spirit. They learn to work together so that all succeed. They experience the truth that *the body is a unit, though it is made up of many parts; and though all its parts are many, they form one body* (1 Cor. 12:12).

BEFORE YOU TRAIN

This chapter provides training plans for your Bible ministry staff. First, there is a plan for training department leaders who have never served in this role before. Then there are three training plans geared to specific Bible ministries. The first plan is for workers in VBS and backyard Bible clubs.

The second is for staff members in a day camp program. The third is a modified program for resident family camp. Read all three plans and use them as the basis for developing a training program to meet the specific needs of your staff.

WHEN SHOULD TRAINING BE HELD?

The first training workshop should be six weeks before your Bible ministry program begins. Four workshops, one each week, may be your choice. Or, you might decide that an intensive weekend training conference would best fit into your church schedule and accomplish the needs and goals of your particular Bible ministry.

The First Evangelical Free Church in Fullerton, California successfully uses the weekend idea. Mel Howell, children's pastor at the church, conducts a Friday evening training session for the "rookies." They spend three hours learning about the ministry they will be involved in. The next day (Saturday) veteran staff members join the rookies for an all-day session in which they learn about the program, the schedule, job responsibilities, teaching skills.

WHO WILL CONDUCT THE TRAINING?

Training is usually the responsibility of the person directly in charge of each particular Bible ministry program. The leader may wish to ask for assistance from other church staff members, the pastor or Sunday School leaders.

WHERE SHOULD THE TRAINING BE HELD?

The actual facility you will use for VBS or other Bible ministry is the ideal workshop site. If you will be conducting backyard Bible schools, day camp, family camp or another away-from-the-church activity, plan at least one meeting at the actual site.

WHAT MATERIALS WILL STAFF NEED FOR TRAINING WORKSHOPS?

Secure for each department leader and teacher a teacher and student book (appropriate to age level), a teaching resource and a copy of this book. Also, a craft kit or craft materials and appropriate directions.

Here are some additional suggestions from pastor Mel Howell: give each staff member a folder, color-coded by department, with his or her name on it. In the folder include the following items: a statement of the ministry objectives; a diagram showing exactly where every activity or class will meet (for day camp or other away-from-church activity, include a street map showing route from church to other site); the curriculum components; a detailed schedule; specific job descriptions and helpful tips to maximize each person's effectiveness; a "survival manual" with practical family management ideas, recipes for easy, quick meals, tips for ensuring domestic tranquillity, and suggestions for communicating with one's spouse while involved in the Bible ministry.

WHAT STAFF DO YOU NEED?

Refer to the chapters in this book (see contents) pertaining to the particular Bible ministry program you have selected. Also, see recruiting chapter for job descriptions.

Emphasize the importance of these training workshops to each staff member. Publicize the meetings by mail, telephone, church bulletins, pulpit announcements, flyers and through the department leaders. Inform your staff that these meetings are not general training, but are specific and practical workshops; also, that each member is expected to attend.

Your own enthusiasm is vital! As you prepare for your Bible ministry, see that the plans and programs are consistently remembered in prayer during the Sunday services. When each staff member is chosen, provide a prayer partner in the congregation—someone who cannot work in the program but who each day will uphold that staff member and the Bible ministry program in prayer.

THREE TRAINING SESSIONS FOR NEW DEPARTMENT LEADERS

When recruiting department leaders (see "Recruiting Your Staff") select people who are committed Christians and who desire to have a loving, caring ministry with adults as well as with children and/or youth. Each potential leader also needs to:
- enjoy helping children or youth learn;
- get along well with adults;
- show organizational skills;
- take initiative.

After your department leaders have been selected and have agreed to serve, plan three training sessions. Because their assignment in leading a VBS department or other summer ministry is a brief one, training must be very specific. Educate your leaders in the actual content and procedures they will be using for their specific Bible ministry.

BEFORE SESSION ONE

For each leader, obtain one set of the appropriate curriculum materials he or she will be using in his or her department; also a copy of this book. Duplicate for each leader two copies of the following job description. You will distribute one copy during *Session One* and the second copy during *Session Three*. Adapt the responsibilities listed in the job description in terms of your particular situation. Leave adequate space on the page for leaders to write examples of each category. Prepare other materials as needed, such as the location of the ministry (with a diagram showing the exact room to be used, or a map for an away-from-church location); a detailed schedule if one is not included in the teaching materials or if you are altering it; copies of music that will be used (if not printed in curriculum materials); a sample of the craft materials you plan to use, if department leaders will be helping to supervise crafts. Following is your job description:

1. Lead group time.
2. Encourage teachers.
3. Suggest changes tactfully.
4. Share materials and equipment.
5. Listen to teachers' problems and suggestions.
6. Assist teachers when necessary.
7. Conduct (or assist with) teacher training sessions.

Session Two will consist of a guided observation experience. Arrange for leaders to observe one or more of your most effective Sunday School leaders, preferably in the same age level in which the new leader will be working.

DURING SESSION ONE

1. Distribute curriculum materials. Read through the daily schedule step-by-step with leaders to identify the specific responsibilities of each one.

2. Assign leaders to read the chapters "How Do They Learn?" and "What Are They Like?" Remind them to answer discussion questions included in the material.

3. If leaders are to be involved in teacher training and/or recruiting procedures (see chapters "Recruiting Your Staff" and "Training Your Staff") review their responsibilities.

4. Explain that *Session Two* will be an observation experience. Distri-

bute one copy of the job description to each leader. Tell each leader the date, time and location for his or her observation session. Suggest that the job description be used as an observation guide. Beside each task on the page ask leaders to write the way the leader being observed demonstrates the task. (**Note:** not every item on the job description will necessarily be observable on a given Sunday.)

5. Ask leaders to carefully review curriculum materials (particularly the group time) before *Session Three.*

6. If department leaders will help supervise crafts, distribute samples and ask leaders to familiarize themselves with the craft before *Session Three.*

BEFORE SESSION TWO

Check with Sunday School leaders to be sure they are expecting observers in their departments.

DURING SESSION TWO

Leaders use job description observation sheets as they observe Sunday School department leaders.

BEFORE SESSION THREE

Familiarize yourself with one of the group time sections from the curriculum. Plan to roleplay the group time at the training session. You or an experienced leader will assume the leader's role; the leaders will assume the role of students.

DURING SESSION THREE

1. Review with leaders their *Session Two* observation notes. For example, ask, "What did the leader you observed do to make group time a valuable learning experience for the students?" "What did the leader do to assist teachers during class time?" "How did the leader encourage teachers?"

2. Give each leader the additional copy of the job description. Go through it section by section, using the following suggestions.

Lead Group Time: Guide leaders in learning the songs they will be using in group time. Then roleplay a group time. You or an experienced leader will model the leader's role. Others will pretend to be students.

Encourage Teachers: Ask leaders to suggest ways to encourage a teacher who is doing a good job handling a student who constantly interrupts. Here is one example: "Susan, I know having Kevin in your class is difficult. But I noticed how well you handle his interruptions. You are doing a super job!"

Suggest Changes Tactfully: In this example, the teacher is doing for the child what he could do for himself. Have leaders offer ways to suggest change tactfully. (Possible answer: "Marge, it seems to me we have to hurry to get through our schedule of activities. Have you felt rushed?. . . I have been thinking of ways we can have a more relaxed atmosphere in our room. I'm wondering if we can let children do more for themselves. Of course their work won't be adult-perfect! We don't expect that. Do you have a child in your class that you feel could handle more of his or her work?")

Share Materials and Equipment: State the situation: Paul has an unexpectedly large class. Karen has a smaller one. The area assigned to Paul's class is inadequate due to the unexpectedly large enrollment. Ask leaders for suggested solutions.

(Example: After the session, leader talks with teachers about ways to ease the crunch in Paul's class. Since Karen has more space than she needs, she agrees to exchange areas with Paul.)

Listen to Teacher's Problems and Suggestions: State the problem: Harvey has been late the last few days for his assignment as a VBS teacher. How should John, the department leader, handle the situation? (Example: As Harvey talks to John about his problems with tardiness, John listens carefully, keeping eye contact with Harvey. John periodically reflects Harvey's comments—"I know from firsthand experience how unexpected things pop up"—to make sure Harvey feels he understands the problem.)

Assist Teachers as Necessary: State the problem: During class time, the department leader sees a visitor who is having difficulty finding Bible references. Ask leaders for suggestions. (Example: Leader quietly sits down beside the student and shows him how to locate the appropriate passage.)

3. Review with leaders the Bible teaching/learning aims, Bible verses and Bible content of each lesson in the curriculum. Also, lead a discussion of the questions included in the chapter "How Do They Learn?" If leaders will be involved in the craft project, make sure they understand how to construct it.

4. Assure leaders you will be praying for them each day and that you are available to assist them in their leadership assignment. Help them feel you are eager to know how they are progressing.

5. Dismiss with prayer.

During VBS or other summer ministry, periodically talk with your leaders to determine their response to their assignments and to offer help with any questions or problems that have arisen.

YOUR TRAINING PLAN FOR VBS, BACKYARD BIBLE CLUBS

WORKSHOP ONE
General Session

Have the recorded VBS theme song (or other appropriate music) playing as group gathers.

Welcome the staff. Begin on time by enthusiastically singing the VBS theme song several times. Express appreciation for those who have come to prepare for their important part in the Bible ministry.

Present the pastor. His enthusiastic five-to-seven minute message should encourage workers to pray and prepare well for their opportunities to introduce children, youth and adults to the Lord Jesus Christ and help them grow by studying His Word together.

Pray together. Pray together in small groups or by department. Thank God for His Son Jesus, the loving Saviour and living Lord.

Introduce the course. Show the VBS filmstrip which describes the Bible study curriculum each department will be using. (Filmstrip available free from your church supplier. Reserve it well in advance.) Or, assign someone to show and briefly describe the theme-related materials. If you prefer, the leader of each department can present these materials during the departmental session.

Outline the schedule. Distribute copies of the schedule indicating the daily activities, room assignments, special activities and any notes on other details.

Introduce the staff. Introduce each staff member and special coordinators. Briefly explain their general responsibilities.

Describe missions emphasis. Have the missions coordinator describe the missionary project selected for your particular Bible ministry and tell how each department will participate. If the departments are involved in individual projects, have the missions co-chairman from each department meet with the missions chairman at the end of this general session for a briefing on the departmental projects. In the remaining workshops the missions co-chairman in each department will assist in working out details for the missionary project with department leader and workers.

Dismiss workers for department session in the areas they will actually occupy during VBS.

Department Session

Take roll and check staff assignments to be sure every job is filled and everyone knows what his or her job is.

Discuss the schedule. If your schedule is different from the one in the VBS teacher's book, duplicate copies of the schedule for all workers.

Discuss, "How Do They Learn?" (see contents) in terms of your particular age level. Use discussion starter ideas suggested in the chapter.

Distribute the teaching materials. Each teacher should have a teacher's manual, student's book and all necessary teaching resources. If all the teachers will be helping in the craft-time projects, each one should receive a craft kit his or her department will be using. Discuss how the projects can be used to help the children learn Bible truths. Encourage teachers to complete samples of the projects before VBS begins.

Give the teachers assignments for Workshop Two. Suggest that all teachers:

1. Read through the teacher and student books to become familiar with the course they will be teaching. Also, ask teachers to jot down examples of activities (suggested in teacher book) which illustrate ways children learn (listed in the "How Do They Learn?" chapter).

2. Read about the age characteristics of the students they will be teaching. (See contents, "What Are They Like?") Also jot down situations from previous experiences or from incidents in their homes or neighborhoods which illustrate various characteristics. Be prepared to discuss the characteristics and illustrations at the next workshop.

WORKSHOP TWO

Meet in age-level departments for the entire workshop.

Learn new music. The department leader (or person responsible for the music) helps the group become familiar with the songs listed in your teacher's manual. Remember, the best way to learn and enjoy new songs is to sing them together several times. When the teachers know the songs and sing them heartily, children and youth will quickly and eagerly join in.

Discuss age characteristics and session aims. List on a flipchart the aims of each session (refer to the aim at the beginning of each session in the teacher's manual), one lesson aim per page. Briefly discuss the age characteristics of the children you will be teaching and how each session aim applies to their everyday experiences.

If your group will include children of varying ages, discuss ways to take into account differences in abilities and needs. (See "Backyard Bible School" chapter of this book for suggestions.) Also, consider together how some lesson aims may need modifying to meet the needs of individual students' abilities and interests. For example, some students may be unfamiliar with the Bible and will even need to learn that we refer to it as God's Word; that God told men what He wanted them to write; that we believe the Bible is true. Others will need to learn how to locate the books of the Bible so they can use their Bibles and participate in each day's Bible study activities. (Because this is often a problem among churched as well as unchurched children and youth, you may want to have available several sets of "How to Use Your Bible" cards [G/L Publications]—available from your church supplier—to help students learn how to use their Bibles.)

Encourage workers to share experiences from their teaching or with their own children which illustrate the general characteristics of the age group(s) they will be guiding in this Bible ministry program. Specific illustrations will be especially helpful to teachers who have not previously worked with this age level.

Assignment. Ask two teachers to volunteer to teach lessons 1 and 2 of your department's course at the next workshop. Emphasize that they will not be "on trial" to see what kind of teachers they are. Rather, this will be a learning experience for both teachers and "students." If the teachers seem reluctant to volunteer, offer to teach the first lesson yourself.

Spend time in prayer together.

WORKSHOP THREE

Meet in age-level departments for the entire workshop. Begin by singing the music you learned last week.

Discuss the Bible memory plans; decide how you will handle this part of your daily program. In the school-age departments appoint one staff member to help children understand and to hear them repeat their memory verses. Designate a quiet area of the department for this important learning activity. Your teacher's manual will suggest ways you can motivate and guide the students as they memorize.

Have the class teachers who volunteered last week practice-teach lessons 1 and 2 from your curriculum. This practice teaching will be a learning experience for everyone. The teacher learns from the experience of actually preparing and teaching the lesson as well as from the comments and suggestions of the other teachers. These teachers, in turn, learn by assuming the role of students during the lesson. They will need to think of ways children may respond to the Bible study and watch for strong and weak points in the teaching.

Important and helpful as it is, practice teaching may be an uncomfortable experience for teachers, especially those who have never taught before. If you practice-teach the first lesson yourself, lead an honest, open discussion and analysis of your teaching. As the workers evaluate your teaching, they will see how helpful the experience can be and become increasingly willing to participate themselves.

The evaluation time that follows the practice teaching is just as important as the actual teaching itself. Be positive and kind in your comments. Begin by asking the practice teachers to express what they will probably do differently when they teach this lesson the next time.

Make the discussion frank and open enough to be of real profit to the teacher and the "students," without hurting feelings. Ask "students" to pick out the good points of the lesson. Also, require entire group to suggest solutions for every problem they identify. Require a positive suggestion with each point of criticism.

Above all, emphasize that this is a "team" experience. The teacher is not trying to "show how it should be done," nor are the students merely trying to criticize or catch the teacher's errors. Rather, all are learning together how to be more effective teachers. Emphasize this approach to the practice teaching. Here are some suggested questions to guide "students" in their observation and discussion.

1. How well did the lesson accomplish the lesson aims?

2. Did the teacher maintain good eye contact with the students?

3. Did the teacher use words and expressions students of this age will understand?

4. Did the introduction to the Bible story capture your attention?

5. What was the "point" or application? Was it expressed throughout the lesson? Or, was it merely tacked on at the end as a "moral"?

6. Did the teacher do most of the talking? Or, did he or she also involve the students in meaningful, interesting Bible learning activities?

At this workshop, or as an assignment before Workshop Four, have each worker complete a student's activity book in order to become familiar with every part of it. Discuss how the Bible study activities in the student's book relate to the lesson aims. Assign one or two teachers to lead the group in this activity, just as you had them practice-teach the lesson.

Assignment. Ask each staff member to read, "Leading a Child to Christ" (see contents).

Close the workshop by introducing the recreation leader. Have him or her lead in some of the games and other recreational activities you will be using in your Bible ministry program. If the class teachers will not be involved in the recreation program, have the recreation staff meet separately to plan and learn the games and activities.

WORKSHOP FOUR
General Session

Sing the VBS theme song and any other songs you'll be using.

For a brief period of time discuss matters of general concern to the entire staff:

Safety. Introduce the person who will be in charge of first aid, and have that person explain the basic procedures to follow in case of an accident or emergency.

Transportation. Introduce the transportation coordinator and have her or him briefly explain any transportation procedures and regulations.

Insurance and Parent Permission Slips. Discuss insurance coverage as it applies to your program both on and off the church property. Distribute copies of the Parent Permission Form (see contents for sample form), and explain its importance; also name the activities or trips which will require such a form. Explain when the forms will be distributed and who will collect them.

Registrar and Records. Introduce the VBS registrar, who will describe the record system you will be using. Distribute samples of the registration cards, attendance forms, and other record materials used for the program. Emphasize the importance of keeping an accurate record system and how it will be used in a follow-up program and in planning for next year's program.

Supplies. Introduce your supply coordinator and have him or her give any necessary instructions regarding the ordering and distribution of supplies. Explain where the supplies will be located and the kinds of materials available.

Follow-up. Describe your plans for follow-up after the Bible ministry program is over, calling special attention to ways the teachers will be involved. Read the chapter, "Following-Up and Evaluating" for help in planning your follow-up program.

Department Session

If you didn't complete the student's activity book discussion at the last session, do this now.

Discuss, "Leading a Child to Christ." Unless teachers know and understand the simple biblical steps, they are apt to overlook a child's readiness to believe in Jesus Christ.

The age at which a boy or girl grasps the meaning of personal salvation depends on his training and background. At this session the school-age departments may want to roleplay a situation in which you, the leader, are leading a child to Christ.

Ask one of the teachers to play the role of the child. ("Leading a Child to Christ" offers instructions for leading a child who is ready to trust the Lord as Saviour.) As the teachers observe the roleplay situations and listen to the discussion and the way you use Scripture verses, they will gain confidence in this area. Many children and youth accept Christ during a VBS or camping ministry, so each staff member needs to be ready to share Christ.

As you conclude the final workshop session and the staff has begun to assimilate all they have learned during the past four sessions, challenge them to:

• Rededicate their lives to Jesus as Lord.

• Look around and see what great things there are to praise God for.

• Begin each day of their Bible ministry with a song of praise to the King of all the earth.

• Show their love and praise for Jesus the Lord. Then their joy will be seen and captured and reflected by the children they lead.

YOUR TRAINING PLAN FOR A DAY CAMP

After these four training workshops, schedule and plan a special "practice day" for the staff to put the total program into practice.

WORKSHOP ONE

Welcome the staff members by expressing the importance of each one; help the staff know that the success of the program depends on their dedication and ministry. Have song leaders (with guitars) ready to involve staff in singing several songs that will be used during the program.

Invite the senior pastor to give a challenge to the staff, stressing the importance of this type of unique ministry. Pray together in small groups, thanking the Lord for this opportunity to express His love and His word.

Define goals. Use a flipchart or an overhead projector to record the goals staff members formulate. Begin by asking, "What are our reasons for having a day camp Bible ministry?" Be sure the list includes, "to increase a camper's understanding of God and His Word through Bible study; to offer opportunities to respond to Jesus' love; to develop in-depth relationships between counselors and campers."

Outline the schedule. (See contents for "Day Camp.") Distribute copies of schedule indicating daily and special activities; also other necessary information.

Introduce staff. As you call each name, briefly explain his or her responsibility.

Discuss, "How Do They Learn?" (see contents) in terms of the particular age levels of children in your day camp. Use discussion starter ideas suggested in the chapter.

Show VBS filmstrip which describes Bible study curriculum each department will be using. (Filmstrip available free from your church supplier. Reserve it well in advance.)

Distribute Bible teaching materials. Each person should have a teacher's manual, student's book, a copy of this book and all necessary teaching resources.

Give counselors assignments for Workshop Two. (Use assignment listed at the conclusion of Workshop One for VBS staff.)

WORKSHOP TWO

Music. Begin Workshop Two by singing songs you will be using in each day of camp. The children will especially enjoy the music if you can use guitar accompaniment.

Discuss age characteristics in terms of the age levels of the children in your program. Talk about the implications these characteristics have for each part of your daily schedule (Bible study, craft experiences, recreation, etc.). Also, discuss ways to prevent possible behavior problems, i.e., provide challenging experiences to forestall boredom (and thus misbehavior); watch for opportunities to relate to children on a one-to-one basis; select activities that are not too difficult or too easy, so each child feels genuinely successful; be sure each child knows rules, i.e., no one leaves camping area without permission; each person cleans up after completing a project, eating lunch, etc.

Discuss Bible teaching material in terms of the aims stated at the beginning of each lesson. Talk over the possible need for modifying the aims in terms of camper's needs and abilities. For example, since children's Bible skills vary, consider using the *"How to Use Your Bible"* cards (available from your church supplier). These materials help children learn individually to locate books of the Bible, references, etc.

Introduce nature specialist to guide counselors in learning such skills as marking a nature trail; outdoor cooking; bird, insect and animal identification.

Introduce craft coordinator who demonstrates craft projects. Divide staff into two groups to make craft samples.

For Workshop Three assignment, ask two counselors to volunteer to practice-teach lessons 1 and 2 from the Bible study materials. Be sure they know they are not expected to perform perfectly; rather, the demonstration will be a learning experience for both teachers and students. If counselors seem reluctant to volunteer, offer to teach lesson 1 yourself.

Spend time in small groups praying together.

WORKSHOP THREE

Review music. Begin by reviewing and learning songs you'll use.

Present demonstration. Have the two counselors who volunteered at the last workshop practice-teach lessons 1 and 2 from your curriculum. (See VBS Workshop Three for suggestions in guiding and evaluating the demonstration.)

Explain mission emphasis. Have missions coordinator describe project selected for your group; also tell how children will participate.

Plan special activities. If your schedule includes such activities as trips or overnight outings, let the staff help plan the events. You may want to include a wiener roast, family picnic or fireside time as a closing program for campers to share highlights of their experiences. Also, be sure all staff members know their particular areas of responsibility.

Assign entire staff to read "Leading a Child to Christ" (see contents). Give each staff member time to practice with another in using the Scriptures and explanation suggested in that chapter. Also, staff members will profit from experience of using the booklet *God Wants You to Be a Member of His Family* (see "Resources") with each other.

Conclude with time of prayer. Thank God for the opportunity to help children know of His love and His Word.

WORKSHOP FOUR

Review music. Sing all songs to be used in your program.

Discuss matters of general concern to entire staff. Include safety, first aid, transportation, insurance and parent permission slips, registrar and records, supplies and follow-up. (For details on these topics, see VBS Workshop Four.)

Guide a discussion on leading a child to Christ. Use *God Wants You to Be a Member of His Family* and the chapter "Leading a Child to Christ" in this book as a basis for discussion. Encourage staff to share experiences from their work with children. Specific illustrations will be especially helpful to staff members who have not had previous experience in leading a child to the Lord. Then pair off the group. Have one person assume the role of a child as the other person demonstrates how to lead a child to Christ, using the Scriptures suggested. Then have the people reverse roles so both may have the opportunity to practice. Each person evaluates the other's approach and gives suggestions that might be helpful.

Plan a "practice day" at the location of your day camp. There the entire staff can put into action the procedures they've been planning. Invite staff members' children, their friends and children in your Sunday School.

Conclude by reviewing briefly your Bible ministry's goals *and objectives.* Challenge staff members to rededicate their lives to the Lord Jesus, to praise Him for the opportunity to share His love with children. Divide into small groups for a brief time of praying together.

YOUR TRAINING PLAN FOR A FAMILY CAMP

The number (and responsibilities) of staff members will be determined by the number and sizes of the families registered and by the ages of their children. Plan for a counselor and assistant for each group of eight to ten children who are age four through second grade. Plan for a counselor and assistant for each group of ten to twelve children who are third grade and older. Provide one baby-sitter for every three children under four years of age. For a list of other staff members, see "Recruiting Your Staff."

The staff members you select need to have a commitment to a ministry to families—helping families realize their God-given potential to be the loving, caring and nurturing units He intended. Staff members also need to have an understanding of the basic goals and program content of family camp (see "Family Camp" chapter in this book). They also need to be aware of age-level characteristics in order to have realistic behavior expectations.

Help staff members begin preparation for their responsibilities as soon as you recruit them. Briefly explain your goals and the main features of the program, defining the duties each person will have. Assign each staff member to prepare for the first training meeting by reading Scriptures that deal with family living (Deut. 6:4-9; Ps. 133; Matt. 12:25; Col. 3:12-21). Also, assign each staff member to read a book or magazine articles, such as *Heaven Help the Home; You, the Parent;* or *Family Life Today* magazine (see "Resources") to aid in understanding some of the realities of family living.

Before the first training meeting. Review the interest finders (see "Family Camp" chapter) registered families have completed. Compare these expressions of family needs with your basic goals and your program schedule. On a flipchart letter the basic goals you want to see accomplished during the time at camp. (See "Family Camp" chapter.) Beside each goal, list a specific program feature that will help accomplish that goal. Also, prepare a copy of program schedule for each staff member.

At the first training meeting. Help staff get acquainted by having each one tell (briefly) his or her family camp duties. Divide into groups of three or four to discuss the assigned Scriptures concerning families. Ask each group to list the kinds of family problems these Scriptures recognize, then list the appropriate action the Bible suggests. Bring groups together to review the interest finders from registered families. Then use flipchart to present the basic goals and the programs planned to help accomplish these goals. Show how each goal reflects the scriptural admonition and meets some of the needs expressed by families on interest finders. Distribute and discuss each part of the schedule, relating the activities to your goals, the Scriptures and the family needs.

Before your second training session. Provide each staff member with material to be used when family groups are combined. (See "Resources.")

At this session. Acquaint the staff with the content and procedures of these parts of the schedule. Actually have staff members work through part of the schedule, such as a discussion time and a family project.

Guide a discussion on assigned books and articles staff has been reading on family living. Talk together about ways staff can use this information. Also discuss importance of attitudes. For example, staff members need to avoid being judgmental toward the varied life-styles of families (i.e., one family may feel very comfortable wearing clothing another family or the counselor might consider inappropriate).

The third training session. This session should be primarily for the age-level leaders to meet for planning their program responsibilities. (Adapt VBS training session procedures.) Each leader will need samples of all materials he will be using. The experiences planned for each age group should reinforce the activities in which the total group will be involved.

Include time for problem solving by staff members. Brainstorm a list of "What if . . ." situations for staff members to discuss: "What if a child disrupts the Bible study?" "What if a teenager refuses to join a discussion?" "What if a fight breaks out?" "What if some of the younger children get restless and noisy during the Family Campfire, and their parents don't control them?" Agree on the best procedures to follow in each case. Then, select several "What if . . ." situations for staff members to roleplay. Set the scene by providing some background information for each roleplay. Ask participants how they think they will react in the situation, then allow them a few moments to think through the role before proceeding. Stop the roleplay after several minutes and discuss what happened.

Let participants express how they felt during the situation. Discuss whether or not the problem was really resolved. What specific things did the "counselor" do that helped resolve it? Did the "counselor" add to the problem in any way? What other things could the "counselor" have done? Give each person at least one opportunity to participate and be evaluated. Keep the emphasis positive, stressing the value of group interaction in practicing for problems before they occur.

The final staff meeting. The fourth session should be held at the campsite, if possible. If it is not practical for the staff to visit the site before the camp dates, arrange for them to arrive at least several hours before families do. This will allow a briefing on facilities, equipment, materials and regulations which will save many possible problems during the camp itself.

Chapter 10

Choosing Your Bible Study Curriculum

An important part of your Bible ministry is the curriculum you choose. You'll need to select your Bible study materials, crafts, nature study materials, music, and other resources with certain criteria in mind. The guidelines in this chapter will aid you in choosing those materials most appropriate to your needs.

OVERALL APPEARANCE

Will the materials appeal visually to the teachers and staff as well as learners for whom they are intended? Do the teacher's and students' books look inviting?

If the materials include promotion items such as buttons, posters, bumper stickers or whatever—will these materials also appeal visually to the people for whom they are intended? Will they attract the unchurched (if you're trying to reach unchurched) as well as church people?

CONTENT

Is the Bible presented as the Word of God in the Bible study materials? Is Jesus Christ honored as the living Word? Is the Bible material appropriate for the age group indicated? Will the material help you accomplish the goals you have chosen for your ministry? For example, if you want to encourage Christian maturity or enrich the Bible knowledge of your learners, will the materials help? If you want to reach the unsaved, do the materials have an outreach thrust, and do they present the gospel simply and clearly? Do the materials provide information only, or do they also provide opportunities for specific behavior changes (i.e., help Christians to grow in Christ; challenge unbelievers to make a commitment to Christ)?

In many seasonal ministries, craft and nature materials can provide meaningful and creative activity. In selecting craft and nature resources, make sure the contents are within leader's or teacher's understanding. (No advanced botanical textbooks!) Will the materials consistently and realistically involve the students in appreciating and understanding interesting facets of God's creation? Are the activities appropriate to the age level of the student? Can the children actually complete almost all the work of the craft projects by themselves? Will the crafts reinforce the aims of the Bible lessons?

What about materials? Some crafts provide almost everything needed to complete the project(s). If you're dealing with instructions-only kind of craft books, ask yourself about the availability of necessary materials, and how much they will cost.

TEACHER MATERIALS

Are the teachers' books easy to follow? Are the teaching methods appropriate for each age group? Will the activities involve the students in life-changing Bible learning experiences? How many staff people does the material call for?

STUDENT MATERIALS

Are the student books attractive? Are the stories, information and directions written in the learner's vocabulary? Are the Bible learning activities appropriate for the learner's age group and abilities? Do the learning activities allow the student to be an active participant in discovering what God's Word says and in putting Bible truth into his or her everyday experiences?

MUSIC

Whatever music you plan to use—be it a few songs each day at VBS, or a complete chorale for a touring choir—ask yourself these questions to guide your choice: Are the words biblically sound? Are they stated in understandable language? Are they appropriate to the understanding of the intended singers or audience?

Is the music appropriate to the words? Is the music within the capabilities of the singers? Will it appeal to the participants and to the audience? (Consider the tastes and convictions of the intended participants and audience; avoid imposing an extremely contemporary program on people who feel comfortable only with traditional hymns; nor do you want to bore a contemporary-minded audience with an unvaried program of music from another era. If your audiences will be varied, consider having a varied program.)

The heart of your Bible ministry is teaching the Word of God. Plan the Bible study activities and songs to give your teaching staff many opportunities to share what God has to say to each person.

OTHER CONSIDERATIONS

Does the material provide teacher training? If so, will it meet the needs of your staff?

Are supplementary materials provided? These might include an organizational handbook, special guide for the director, promotional materials such as posters, flyers, doorknob hangers, and so on.

Is the material based on five or ten days, or are both plans available?

What is the cost of the material?

Are there any special features? (One curriculum may be available in Spanish, another may provide instructions for adapting the lessons for mentally retarded children or for urban churches; some may provide special music or an emphasis on social concerns.)

Chapter 11

Publicizing Your Program

FOUR VITAL STEPS

Before you formulate a promotional program for your Bible ministry program, carefully think through these steps:

1. *Identify the people you want to reach.* Effective advertising uses a rifle, not a shotgun. Aim at "everybody" and you'll probably hit no one. Narrow the target down to the exact people you are most anxious to reach and your efforts will probably be effective.

For example, if your promotional goal is to inform the neighborhood children about your Bible ministry program, then select your advertising or publicity vehicles with that aim in mind. ("Advertising" usually means time, space or equipment you pay for; "publicity" usually means the media that cost you nothing.) Consider the promotional means available to you which in a unique way speak to the children of this age group.

2. *Describe the results you are aiming for.* Once you have identified the people you want to reach, you will need to decide what you want them to do. People respond best to a precise, definite challenge to act, rather than vague generalities. Perhaps you want them to give you their name and address for a mailing list, or you want their registration for your VBS or other ministry. If you want such a response, you must (1) provide a *response mechanism*—coupon, business reply card, etc.—and (2) provide

some *motivation* that will cause them to act. Often the simple appeal of the program itself is adequate motivation, but sometimes you will need to offer a special prize or reward to motivate the desired response.

But don't do anything until you have identified your target audience and clearly defined your advertising goals. Discipline yourself to come back to these goals frequently to be sure your promotional activities are "on target."

3. *Select the media that will reach your audience and accomplish your purpose.* Not all the so-called "mass media" will be available to you for your Bible ministry, but give serious consideration to newspapers, radio, television, billboards, telephone and direct mail. You'll want to add to the list several other possibilities: bus cards, door-to-door throwaways, posters, bumper stickers, placards, etc. Let your imagination run wild; and don't be afraid to borrow ideas from the commercial advertising "experts" who are competing for your own attention!

In promoting children's activities, you need to reach two audiences: the children themselves and their parents. So, you'll need to use several different media. The comic section of the Sunday paper is an obvious means of reaching the children. No, you probably can't put an ad in the comics. But you may be able to make a deal with the person who delivers the comics! Get in touch with your neighborhood carriers and find out what they'd charge to insert your printed message in the comic section of the Sunday paper. (Be sure this doesn't violate the policies of the publisher.) With a little humor and creativity, you'll be able to reach practically every child in your community within half a day.

4. *Plan the best, most effective ways to get and hold your target-persons' attention while communicating your message to them.* It's not always easy to distinguish between the media that you use and the devices you employ to get people's attention and hold their interest. But bear in mind that the mere choice of newspaper advertising as being best to reach your target people does not mean you've scored any points. There is good newspaper advertising and there is bad. Although the use of newspaper advertising may be an excellent way to reach your target audience, a poorly designed or poorly worded ad may be a waste of money.

What will get the attention of a child and hold his interest? All kinds of ideas will come to mind: parades, costumes, comic books, games, music. Does that brief list suggest any possibilities for advertising material? Keep thinking, and a dozen other suggestions will come to mind.

One church got some interesting results from a neighborhood dog parade to advertise its day camp. Several of the Sunday School kids got together and walked their dogs on leashes carrying signs inviting other children to "bring your pooch to day camp at Calvary Church." The church then provided a special place where dogs could be tied or penned during the day. Plenty of water was made available, along with a bag of bones furnished by the local supermarket. Several breaks were scheduled during which the children could admire each other's pets. If a "dog day" turns out to be impractical, you can open up a new list of possibilities with cats, rabbits, gerbils or even goldfish...or *all* of them!

You'll also need to consider "interior" promotion—your efforts to reach your own people within the congregation and get them involved in your Bible ministry.

Many people who plan a Bible ministry assume that their own people know the details and already plan to participate. However, people *aren't* always listening when you tell them about the coming attractions. They don't always read the announcements in the church bulletin, and they aren't as attentive as they ought to be to the notices on the board in the hall. So "spell it out" plainly, and repeat it several times.

Your mimeograph or ditto machine is a great tool for reaching members and adherents—or you might try the services of a nearby "quick print" shop. A 5½x8½ inch page makes a good bulletin insert, and you can design one to fit your own needs. If your goal is recruiting workers for VBS or other Bible ministry, be sure to use some sort of response device—like a "yes, count on me to help..." coupon at the bottom of the page.

An almost sure winner in building enthusiasm is a poster contest in which suitable awards are offered for the best creations by Sunday School children at various age levels. The kids can come up with an amazing assortment of ideas, and putting these ideas into tangible form assures their own interest. The presence of their posters in strategic spots around the church building and community will help toward getting attention (and results) for the event you are publicizing.

Be sure to use pictures of your past Bible ministry activities in your publicity. Ask the skilled amateurs or the professional photographers in your church to record on film interesting events to use in publicizing your next Bible ministry. Pictures draw people and are a valuable publicity tool.

TWENTY-THREE PROMOTIONAL IDEAS

1. VBS FILMSTRIP
Some VBS curriculum publishers offer a sound/color filmstrip to moti-

vate workers and describe the teaching materials. You may borrow or buy the filmstrip from your VBS supplier. Be sure you reserve the filmstrip well before you need it, for your supplier will have many requests for its use.

2. BULLETIN INSERTS

Make up a colorful promotional flyer for a church bulletin insert. Use these inserts twice: once to recruit staff members and again on the Sunday before your Bible ministry begins.

On staff recruitment Sunday, reproduce the following message on the back of the inserts:

This (summer) our church is going to help children and young people discover the Lord Jesus. You can be a part of this exciting Bible ministry. Fill out the information requested below, indicating your desire to serve as a teacher, assistant, craft leader, secretary, pianist or any of the several other positions. Then place this flyer in the offering plate or give it to one of our ushers. You'll be contacted regarding the important part you can have in our Bible ministry.

YES! I want to help in our church's Bible ministry. I'm willing to serve in the _____ as a _____ .
Signed: _____
Address: _____
Phone: _____
(List the kinds of Bible ministries your church is sponsoring, with the positions open in each ministry.)

---

3. PRE-SUMMER RALLY

About two weeks before public school concludes, hold a pre-summer rally on a week night or a Sunday evening. Invite all Sunday School students, parents and friends, plus neighborhood children and their parents. Feature a special children's speaker, movie or other attraction. Describe the various kinds of summer ministries you will be conducting, and distribute promotional information. Have the registration booth open (see no. 16) for those who want to preregister on the spot.

4. POSTCARDS

Colorful postcards featuring the theme are available from your VBS supplier. Reproduce an invitation message on the back and mail them to all prospective students, including your entire Sunday School enrollment. Or, give the Sunday School teachers a supply of cards and ask them to add personal messages and mail the cards to their students. Use the postcards to recruit staff members.

5. DISPLAYS

About three months before VBS begins, arrange a display of the teaching materials as a part of your staff recruitment program. Include visual teaching tools, teacher's and students' books, completed craft projects and other materials that will demonstrate to the prospective workers the many helps available to them.

6. BULLETIN ANNOUNCEMENTS

Your regular Sunday church bulletin is probably the most widely-read publicity piece your church has. Use it regularly. Announce key staff appointments as soon as they are confirmed. When you have settled on the dates for your various Bible ministries, share this information with your entire congregation via the bulletin. Publicize your staff training workshops, your need for cookies or craft materials, transportation needs, the prayer partner program.

7. ANNOUNCEMENTS IN CHURCH

Ask your pastor (or other person who makes the announcements in church services) to emphasize your Bible ministry during the two or three weeks before it begins. In addition to this type of announcement, consider having testimonies from staff and students who benefited from the ministry last year. Or let teachers and students have a brief parade through the sanctuary. They can carry placards promoting the theme, pictures from the teaching resources, crafts, balls to be used during recreation time, and other items related to the Bible ministry.

8. ANNOUNCEMENTS IN SUNDAY SCHOOL

Make sure your Bible ministry is enthusiastically promoted in every Sunday School department that will be included in the activities. Show slides or brief movies; have teens prepare skits; show samples of crafts; tell about any special activities such as contests or field trips that the ministry will include.

9. CHILDREN'S SERMON

Ask your pastor to include a children's sermon in your Sunday worship services. Suggest he present a brief talk based on the teaching theme from your Bible ministry. He might also want to use visual materials related to the ministry (such as posters available with VBS curriculum).

10. POSTER CONTEST

About two months before your Bible ministry begins, announce a poster contest for the children and youth who will be involved. Let each student make a poster that illustrates the theme. Allow them to use any art medium they choose: poster paints, crayons, collage, chalk. Emphasize that the posters should not only illustrate the theme, but also feature the name, dates and other important information about the activity itself.

Choose a committee to judge the posters on neatness and originality. Give the contest winners a partial scholarship to camp. Display the posters in the church for a week or two. Then ask local stores and businesses to place the posters in their windows to advertise your Bible ministries. Use *all* posters, not just the winners.

11. ESSAY CONTEST

Let school-age children compete for partial camp scholarships by writing one-page essays based on the teaching theme of your Bible ministry. Publish the winning essay(s) in your local newspaper or church publication as part of the promotional campaign for your Bible ministry. (You might have first, second, and third place winners in each department. Post winning essays on departmental bulletin boards.)

12. T-SHIRT PARTY

Throw a party for the teenagers in your church; each one attending designs a T-shirt illustrating the teaching theme of your Bible ministry. (See *Easy-to Make Crafts for Preteens and Youth* for crayon-on-cloth directions. Available from your church suppliers.) For design ideas, check the promotional materials in your curriculum or review kit.

13. GO-WHERE-PEOPLE-GO SERENADE

Ask a musical group from your choir or youth department to go with sponsors to local recreation areas in your community (lake, beach, park, etc.). Take along flyers promoting your Bible ministry, with complete information. As the musicians stroll about the area serenading people with music from the planned curriculum, distribute flyers, particularly to family groups.

14. NEIGHBORHOOD CANVASS

Four or five weeks before your Bible ministry begins, recruit a crew of visitors from your junior, youth and adult departments. Reproduce an invitation on the backs of promotional flyers. Divide the area you want to cover into two-block sections.

On canvass day (probably a Saturday morning or afternoon two or three weeks before your program begins) divide the volunteers into teams of two. Be sure you have an adult supervisor in each two-block section. Leave a printed invitation to your Bible ministry at each home, with a personal invitation whenever someone is home. Caution your visitors not to place the flyers in mailboxes, as this is against postal regulations. Some curriculum publishers provide publicity material in the form of doorknob hangers; or you can create your own. Unprinted plastic bags may also be used. Cut a slit in each one large enough to fit over a doorknob, then insert your literature. Provide simple refreshments at your church when the canvass is completed.

15. PRINTED THEME POSTERS

Bright, colorful, full-color posters illustrating the theme are available at low cost from your VBS supplier. Buy as many of these posters as you can. Have several of your youth classes come to the church on a Saturday four of five weeks before your program begins for a "poster party." They can letter the name of the church, the activity, dates, and hours on the posters with felt pens, then take the posters to the stores and businesses of your area.

16. REGISTRATION BOOTH

Place a large table or a booth in a heavily traveled part of your church facility during the three or four weeks before your summer program begins.

Cover the outside of the booth with posters (both commercial and handmade), banners, and large cut-out letters advertising the Bible ministries program of your church. Include large photographs of the previous year's activities.

Staff the booth with friendly, outgoing children and young people who will preregister as many students as possible. Provide a generous supply of promotional materials: flyers, buttons, lapel stickers, posters, etc. Call attention to the booth in your church bulletin and public announcements.

If you have a promotional parade, move the registration booth to the parade site and again use it to distribute promotional information and preregister students.

17. LAPEL STICKERS AND BUTTONS

A variety of VBS lapel buttons are available at low cost from your VBS supplier. You can also make your own lapel stickers from self-adhesive labels. The labels come in either rolls or sheets in a variety of bright colors and sizes. Check with your local stationery store for samples.

Distribute promotional buttons or stickers early in your staff recruitment campaign to build interest and enthusiasm. Also distribute them to all Sunday School students a week or two before school is out and encourage them to wear them to school.

18. NEWSPAPER ARTICLES

Most community newspapers are glad to print well-written stories about special activities for children and young people. During the last few weeks before your Bible ministry begins, send two or three interesting stories about your program to the paper. Include glossy finished black-and-white photographs of key leaders, the poster contest winners, or other interesting subjects with your articles. On the back of all photos paste a label giving a description of the photo subject, with names of all people.

The story should feature the who, when, what, where and why of your Bible ministry in the first two paragraphs. Then go on into the details: program features, special attractions, etc. Include a phone number from which interested persons can secure additional information.

The story should be typed, doublespaced, with one-inch margins all around. In the upper left corner of the first page type the words, "For immediate release," or give a future date if you want the story held. Under these words type the name and address of the church. In the upper right corner type your own name and telephone number.

Some VBS curriculum includes sample newspaper stories and advertisements which you can use.

19. PARADE

The weekend before your Bible ministry have a children's parade at a local shopping center. Get permission to use the parking area. Cooperate fully with the manager so you impede the traffic as little as possible.

Have the boys and girls of your Sunday School decorate their bicycles, tricycles and wagons. Attach some posters to long sticks for the children to carry as placards; or they can wear them like sandwich boards. Give each parade participant a supply of flyers to hand out to those watching.

Set up your registration booth or a table decorated with posters and banners advertising your program. Let some of your teenagers preregister people and answer questions. Have several adults in the area of the parade and near the booth.

20. REGISTRATION AND PUBLICITY FAIR

Two weeks before your Bible ministry, hold a preregistration and publicity fair on your church lawn or parking lot, or in the parking lot of a shopping mall. (Check with appropriate personnel.) Place banners and posters in conspicuous locations. Have a puppet show booth presenting simple Bible stories.

Invite a youth choir to become a strolling group, singing songs from the Bible ministry. Plan a booth to introduce your missionary project with samples of food from the country where the missionary serves, plus maps and visual illustrations of the missions project. (Your church missions committee might want to help coordinate this booth.)

Arrange a display of crafts, T-shirts, buttons, posters, and other materials related to the Bible ministry. Plan an area for showing slides of last year's ministry. Have plenty of flyers to give out.

At the registration booth have a supply of registration/attendance cards to use in registering students. Also prepare prayer partner cards, with the name of a Bible ministry staff person on each index card. People interested in being prayer partners take cards and agree to pray daily for the staff member whose name is on each card. Staff people for the ministry can wear lapel buttons or other promotional devices and be available to meet students.

21. AT A FAIR

Participate in county or city fairs by having a booth for your Bible ministry. Attractively arrange curriculum materials, craft projects and missionary artifacts. Distribute flyers, inviting the community to participate in your Bible ministry.

22. TRANSPORTATION ROUTE SIGNS

You can get a little free publicity through your transportation system.

Have your church bus (or the car pool) follow a regular route each day. Designate specific pick-up points where children who need transportation can assemble. Mark these points by mounting theme posters on utility poles or mounting them on sticks driven into the ground. (Be sure such signs are not illegal in your community.)

On the poster letter the following information:

THE WAY

Destination: (name of church or location of activity).
Time: (when pickup will be made at this point).
Dates: (beginning and closing dates of activity).
Return: (time the bus or car will return to this spot).

This information will help parents know when and where their children will be picked up and returned. You will also cut transportation time by making fewer stops. Be sure you remove the signs when your prograram is over.

23. USE LAST YEAR'S ATTENDANCE LISTS

Make a personal contact with everyone who attended your ministry last year.

Publicizing the activities of your Bible ministry is a spiritual ministry—a ministry of reaching out to others. Let God guide your publicity program so that many will come and hear the life-giving message of God's love.

Chapter 12

Closing the Program

One of the highlights of your Bible ministry can be your closing program/open house. This program allows you to get acquainted with the parents of the children who have been attending your Bible ministry. It also gives the children an opportunity to share what they have learned, and provides a bridge between the special Bible ministry and the regular year-round activities of your church.

Some churches hold the closing program on the afternoon or evening of the last day of their VBS or other Bible ministry. Others prefer the evening before the last day, so that the "take home" projects can be distributed on the following day.

Let each department or group arrange its own display of craft projects, students' books and other group projects so the guests can see the good work done.

Plan an open house after the program for guests to visit the various displays. Provide coffee and cookies so the teachers will have time to get better acquainted with the parents.

Include the time and date of the closing program on all announcements concerning your Bible ministries. Let children make the invitations. Send invitations home with the students several days before the program.

Plan a program of not more than an hour and fifteen minutes. Make it a natural outgrowth of the daily accomplishments of each department. Use suggestions of the departmental presentations listed in the teachers' manuals of the curriculum you have used for your ministry.

Chapter 13

Following-up and Evaluating

Effective follow-up begins several weeks before your Bible ministry begins. Appoint a follow-up coordinator and include him or her in every aspect of your planning. Encourage him or her to coordinate all plans with the Sunday School and church visitation and follow-up programs.

Keep accurate records of all students who attend your Bible ministries. Include name, address, church affiliation (if any) and as much information as is practical and helpful about the student's family. (Simple, easy-to-use record cards are available from your VBS supplier.) After your Bible ministry is over, give the record cards to the follow-up coordinator, with notes about any specific decisions the students made or insights into their lives and needs.

Organize a series of special "new convert" classes to help new Christians begin to grow in their life with Christ. The classes may meet during the Sunday School hour, on Sunday evenings, on a week night or Saturday. They are usually conducted at the church, though some leaders prefer the more relaxed atmosphere of a home.

In many cases the teacher or leader who introduced the student to Christ is the logical one to do the follow-up. A relationship already exists that will make follow-up work easier. However, sometimes a close friend or relative who has been praying for the student's conversion is better able to help him grow.

Your follow-up coordinator may want to recruit a staff of people who, though they cannot work in the Bible ministry itself, will commit themselves to a ministry of follow-up beginning while the Bible ministry is still in progress. The coordinator should meet with these people several times to explain how the follow-up program will work, and to show them how to use effective follow-up materials and techniques.

INVOLVE THEM IN SUNDAY SCHOOL

If a student from a non-Christian home makes a decision for Christ, be very discreet in your follow-up. Allow the student himself to tell his parents of his decision—it will help him grow and the parents will probably be more receptive to their child's statement than they would be to the announcement of a stranger.

Encourage children and young people to obey their parents at all times and to set a good Christian example for them, even if the parents oppose their participation in church activities. Never be guilty of fostering disobedience.

One of the best methods of follow-up is to get the student involved in the Sunday School. Arrange for a Sunday School teacher to visit in the home of each prospect or new Christian who is the right age to attend his or her class. If possible, have the student's Bible ministry leader go with the Sunday School teacher.

New Christians aren't the only people who need follow-up work. Many Christian students will make major or minor decisions in their Christian lives during your Bible ministry. Note these decisions on your record cards before you give the cards to the follow-up coordinator. Have him or her talk with the students' Sunday School teachers, youth leaders or others who can help shepherd the students as they begin to live out the decisions they have made.

You may want to set up some special programs for these students. For example, you might begin a Saturday morning discipleship group for young people who have committed their lives to Christian service. Some churches assign an older "big brother" or "big sister" to such students. These people meet with the students informally to encourage and guide them in Christian growth. In such informal relationships students are more likely to open up and share their problems and concerns.

Many students from unchurched homes will attend your Bible ministry. Whether or not they make some specific decision, you'll want to follow them up. Let them and their families know that you would be glad to have them come to your church. And if they ever have a special need or problem, they should feel free to contact you and your pastor.

EVERYONE WHO VISITS

Guidelines for effective visitation that should be followed:

1. If the family attends a Bible-believing church, encourage them to attend regularly even if it's a church not of your denomination. Be extremely tactful and do not downgrade their church by word or attitude, or you'll turn them off completely.

If it seems appropriate, invite them to visit your church and leave attractively printed information about your church with them.

2. If they have not received the Lord as their Saviour, invite the whole family to sit with you as you unfold the good news about Christ and what He did for them. Urge them to receive the free gift of salvation.

Then invite the family to come with you to church next Sunday. "I'll be glad to pick you up at 9:30 next Sunday. How about it?"

Leave information about your church. Before you leave, suggest that you would like to visit them again.

3. Be sure that you communicate sincere interest in them as people, not merely as potential numbers on the church roll. Don't do all the talking. Listen a lot so you can determine their needs and minister to them in those areas.

4. If the parents are not ready to come to your church at this time, tell them about the distinctives of your Sunday School and offer to arrange transportation for their children. You'll find that parents will cooperate because they feel that any moral training their children can get will be good for them.

EVALUATE YOUR BIBLE MINISTRIES

How successful *was* your Bible ministry this year? Did it really accomplish all you intended? Could you have reached more students? Was transportation adequate? Did you have enough teachers and helpers? What about the curriculum materials and crafts? Were they worth the time and money?

Careful evaluation is an important part of any ministry. It not only helps you and your staff recognize success, but also is a valuable guide for an even more successful Bible ministry next year.

Begin your evaluation as soon as your program is over. Mimeograph copies of the Evaluation Questionnaire on the next page and distribute them to all key leaders. An appreciation banquet or potluck dinner honoring all workers (don't forget the custodian!) would be a good time to ask for their written evaluations. Schedule this activity within ten days after your program is over.

As soon as you have collected the evaluation sheets, arrange a meeting with all department leaders. (Allow at least a week for them to study the evaluation sheets before the meeting.) Discuss the evaluation sheets from each department with the leaders. Note both strong and weak areas of the program. Discuss why these areas were strong or weak, and note suggested improvements for next year. In addition to the three areas covered in the evaluation sheet (curriculum, aims/objectives, personnel), consider such matters as these:

Evangelism. How was the plan of salvation presented in each department? Were teachers prepared to explain salvation to their particular age group? Did teachers have time to talk to each student personally about his or her relationship to Christ?

Finance. Were funds adequate to meet expenses? Was money wisely spent? Are complete records of all expenditures available for next year's director? Where could costs have been cut, and where was more money needed? How was stewardship taught to the students?

Publicity. If more than one means of publicity was used, which proved most effective? What other media could have been used to advantage?

Staff recruitment and training. Were staff members appointed early enough? Were they qualified and well prepared? How could you have strengthened your training program? Was more training needed in the use of the curriculum? Schedule? Classroom control? Evangelism?

Transportation. Was transportation sufficient? How could bus (or car) routes be improved next year?

Follow-Up. Were adequate records kept to facilitate follow-up? Were teachers instructed how to visit in homes? Has a follow-up program actually been started? With what results?

Records. Were detailed records kept on enrollment, daily attendance, finances (including cost per student), refreshments (amount served and the cost)? How do these records compare with last year's? Will they be available to help plan for next year's ministry? Where are they filed?

Write or type your evaluation neatly, including comments about any other areas not listed above. File this evaluation with other records in the church or Sunday School office. Next year's director will be grateful for the help provided by such an evaluation.

EVALUATION QUESTIONNAIRE

Name _____

Age or group or Department _____

Type of ministry (VBS, Day Camp, etc.) _____

Careful evaluation is an important part of our work. Will you help by giving your comments about the following areas? Be as specific as possible in your comments. Please return this evaluation sheet by (date).

1. Curriculum

    Were the materials suitable for the age you taught?

    Did you have enough equipment and supplies for effective teaching? What more did you need?

    Were the craft projects valuable? Easy to make? Too time consuming?

2. Goals

    What were your deparment's goals?

    Do you feel your age group/department achieved these goals? In what ways?

    In what ways did you not reach the goals you had set?

3. Personnel

    Did you have enough helpers and teachers in your department? If not, what other workers were needed?

    Was adequate training given in preparation for your work?

    What additions or improvements would you suggest?

4. Was our schedule a realistic one? Did you have enough time for each activity? How could our schedule have been improved?

5. How could we have reached more people?

6. What were our "strong points"? (Be objective and realistic.)

7. What were our "weaknesses"? (Be frank and honest. Avoid personalities.)

8. What other suggestions do you have for improving next year's Bible ministry?

Part IV

Who Are Your Learners?

God has entrusted teachers in the church with opportunities to help them learn vital scriptural truths. An effective teacher is aware of learner's needs, how they grow and develop; also how these processes influence their attitudes and actions—particularly as related to ways they learn best.

Chapter 14

How Do They Learn?

One of the basic aims in every Bible ministry is to help people *learn* effectively. You might want unbelievers to learn that God loves them and offers them redemption. You might want young people to learn several new elements of Christian behavior. You might want adults to learn how God can help them with their problems.

In order to help people learn, you'll need to know *how* they learn. Following are some general principles of learning that apply to all age levels; also some specific age-level examples of ways to implement those principles.

ATTENDING

Attending (listening) is the first step in learning. The teacher must stimulate the learner's interest, thus creating within the learner a desire to learn. Success in securing attention often demands that the teacher begin by presenting an object or a concept familiar and interesting to the learner.

Catching a young child's attention can be easily done by showing him an interesting object (or a picture of the object) or by making a sound. The child then needs to know what he is expected to do with the object, so he must listen to verbal instructions, watch a demonstration of its use or hear a question that caused him to think about what he will do.

Older children usually respond to an interesting variation of a familiar situation or object. For example, one teacher displayed a few very simple origami (paper folding) animals. Children were immediately interested in handling and identifying figures. Youth and adults respond to verbal stimulation, such as being asked to solve several problems a teacher might suggest. For example, "What would you do if it were necessary to steal in order to save a friend's life?"

Discussion Starter: Divide teachers (counselors) according to the age level they will be guiding. Suggest they work in pairs to list four ways (appropriate to learners' age level) to catch learners' attention. Allow five minutes. Then each pair shares with others in age-level group. Allow five minutes. All groups come together again. (Repeat this procedure for each of the subsequent *Discussion Starter* activities.)

EXPLORING

Exploring is the second learning task—the learner's search or investigation of a problem or subject at hand. Learners are explorers, involved in the search for something not yet known or experienced. Their interest must be captured and they are not passive listeners or mere spectators; they are active participants in the teaching/learning process. Their energies need to be directed toward relevant, need-fulfilling goals if learning is to be an adventure. The freedom for learners to choose learning activities in which they are particularly interested and which they enjoy, is especially important to fulfill this learning task adequately.

For example, a young child will eagerly explore the properties of a take-apart toy by removing pieces and examining them. All children are interested in exploring the attributes of colors by working with paint, a prism, tissue lamination, etc. Youth and adults enjoy exploring attractive books and periodicals for new information.

Discussion Starter: Divide groups (as before) to list four activities in which their particular age level will have exploring opportunities.

DISCOVERING

Discovering, the third learning task, culminates the exploring phase of learning. For example, when a teacher of young children cuts open an apple (crosswise) and shows it to the child, the child discovers that the seeds are arranged in a star design. Exploring with colors usually results in a learner discovering that mixing two primary colors produces a secondary color. Learners who search a particular Bible passage to find reasons for

God's commands enjoy discovery when they are able to understand the information they are studying. Discovering truth is particularly exciting for learners as it increases their confidence in their ability to use God's Word and understand its meaning.

Discussion Starter: Again divide group as previously suggested. Suggest teachers list opportunities for discovery they could offer their learners.

APPROPRIATING

Appropriating, the fourth learning task, involves the application to the learners' lives of what they discover. Too frequently our teaching ends with merely an understanding of Bible stories or passages of Scripture without the students really understanding the implications for their own lives. An appropriate question properly timed can often be the tool that leads the student to think about the Bible truth in terms of "What does this mean to *me*?"

For example, at the early childhood level, a teacher's simple questions help a child clarify his thinking about a Bible verse. "Keith, our Bible says, *Be kind to each other.* How can you be kind to your friend Tommy?" Children can relate the kindness of the Good Samaritan to their own experience by telling how they would do likewise in a specific situation. Youth and adults can also state how the Bible principle, *Love your enemies,* can affect their behavior in a competitive situation.

Discussion Starter: Divide groups to list ideas (appropriate to age level) to use in determining if learner has understood ways to apply Bible truth in his day-by-day experiences; also ways to encourage students to tell or illustrate examples of application.

ASSUMING RESPONSIBILITY

Assuming responsibility is the crown and culmination of the learning process. Yet it is often left up to "faith." We hope that what is learned through our stories, discussion, and learning activities will in some way be put into actual practice in the students' lives. But we cannot leave this task up to their initiative (unless they actually suggest ways that they will, on their own, live out the truth). Usually, we need to lead the students to suggest ways in which they can obey the truth they've discovered.

For example, a teacher needs to be consistently alert to situations in which a young child could have a firsthand experience in putting a Bible truth into action. When Susan asked for more clay, Mrs. Lee said to Bobby (who had more than enough), "Susan needs more clay. What could you do to help her?" When Bobby shared clay with Susan, Mrs. Lee reinforced his acceptable behavior with words of praise and encouragement.

Children can plan specific things to do at home or school to demonstrate concern for their family members or friends, then report back at the next session on the results of their efforts. Youth and adults might conduct a group work project as a way to put into practice Bible commands to help those in need. Or they might devise personal plans for changing their attitudes toward another person, in obedience to the command to *love your enemies.*

Discussion Starter: Divide into groups again to list situations a teacher or counselor might create which would encourage the learner to voluntarily think of and do certain actions reflecting a Bible command.

Chapter 15

What Are They Like?

There is a wide range of differences among children. Each child is an individual and develops at his or her own rate. However, there is enough similarity among children of the same age that specific characteristics can be noted. Use these behavior traits as a guide while you plan learning activities for your learners. (See VBS training sessions in "Training Your Staff" for specific ways to use this information.)

PREKINDERGARTNERS (Ages three and four)

PHYSICAL GROWTH

Both three- and four-year-olds are developing large muscle control. However, they still lack sufficient coordination for dependable use of small muscles. So, do not expect these children to cut accurately with scissors or to color within an outline. Have large crayons and sheets of blank paper for draw-and-color activities; dough for squeezing and pounding.

Both threes and fours seem to be constantly on the go—running, jumping, walking or climbing. Provide activities, such as blocks for building (and room to move about!) to encourage the use of large muscles. Keep furnishings to a minimum. Provide a choice of activities and freedom to move from one activity to another.

Provide a fenced, out-of-doors space for climbing, use of wheel toys, digging (if you have a sandbox) and running. Check all equipment for safety—no sharp edges or loose pieces.

Threes and fours play hard and tire easily. Alternate periods of active and quiet play. Be alert to the child who is becoming overstimulated. Tiredness may result in unacceptable behavior. Guide the child to a quiet activity, such as working a puzzle or looking at a picture book with you. During the second hour of your schedule, plan for a rest time of not less than ten minutes.

MENTAL GROWTH

Threes and fours are attentive only as long as they are interested. Their attention span is limited. When children become restless, use songs and finger fun which allow them to move. Alternate listening times with more active experiences. Allow times when children are free to move from one activity to another according to their interest.

Three- and four-year-olds do not understand symbolism! Use simple stories told in literal terms—words that mean exactly what they say. Memory is undependable. Avoid asking, "What was last week's (or yesterday's) story about?" A child also may have difficulty understanding directions. Give one brief direction at a time. Allow the child to complete the task before suggesting the next one.

Threes and fours have a strong desire to learn. They are curious and questioning. Their favorite words seem to be *how, what* and *why*. They learn by doing. Provide materials they can touch, smell, see and even taste. Use lesson-related objects and activities to relate Scripture truths to the child's life.

EMOTIONAL GROWTH

Three- and four-year-olds are sensitive to your actions, attitudes and feelings. Know each child as an individual. You represent God's love to the young child. As you express a genuine interest in him or her as an individual, you are vividly communicating God's love in a way the young child can understand.

Use the child's name often as you talk with him. Listen attentively to what he tells you. When you talk with him, sit or bend down so your face is at his eye level. Give him your undivided attention (stop what you are doing). Respond to his words appropriately by sharing his enthusiasm or offering a bit of sympathy. As you show genuine interest in each child, you are demonstrating God's love in a way the child can understand. The Lord

Jesus' command that we *love one another* (1 John 4:7) becomes alive with meaning. God's Word demonstrated is often more convincing to young children than God's Word explained.

Three- and four-year-olds are testing their world. They may exhibit unacceptable behavior just to see how far they can go. They find security in the very limits they defy; yet they need the security of limits that do not hinder their freedom to experiment. Be consistent in your guidance. Be positive in your suggestions. Emphasize the behavior you desire rather than the kind you want to discourage. Say, "We keep the blocks in the block area" rather than, "Don't bring the blocks to the home corner!" The word "don't" usually makes a child want to resist. Young children may be overaggressive and may use physical force to get what they want. Be alert to the physical safety of all the children.

Young children are keenly aware of the way you handle your Bible; your attitude of prayer and your enthusiasm as you help them know what God's Word says. Your respect and reverence toward the Bible help lay the foundation for children's developing attitudes and feelings toward God's Word.

SOCIAL GROWTH

Three-year-olds enjoy being with other children, but they still like to play alone. They haven't quite left their self-centered "me, my and mine" world. Offer activities that allow them to participate successfully with other children. To help them enjoy their own accomplishments, provide tasks within their abilities. Help strengthen feelings of self-worth by offering words of genuine praise for children's efforts.

Overaggressiveness is noticeable in some three-year-olds. Sometimes this behavior is children's way to gain the attention of adults or other children. Sometimes it's simply caused by lack of experience in working with children their own age. Plan for each child to have some individual attention. Also create opportunities that foster social development. For instance, "Terry, you have lots of pegs. I think John needs more pegs. What can you do to help John?...You are a kind friend to share pegs with John."

Four-year-olds show a growing interest in doing things with other children. They prefer to work in small groups. (Younger fours may still prefer to work alone.) Provide activities that allow the children to work in groups of two or three.

Four-year-olds like to pretend. "I'm the daddy and you're the mother" kinds of play occur frequently in the home living area. These children also like to play out their experiences. "We're going to the park today. Everybody get ready," a four is likely to announce. Provide both men's and women's clothing for dress-up. Include scarves, hats, jewelry, etc. Also provide other materials such as vases, discarded cameras, binoculars, keys, etc.

Moving out into a world of new friends, new activities and experiences, new relationships with adults, means these children need your help. Your thoughtful and careful guidance can help assure their success.

SPIRITUAL GROWTH

Both three- and four-year-olds are trusting and ready to accept what you tell them about God and the Lord Jesus. In conversation and song use Bible truths to assure each child of God's (Jesus') love and care for him. As Sam and his mother rode along home, Sam announced, "God didn't come to Bible school today." After a moment of silence, he added, "But He sent my teacher." To the young child, you represent God's love. Your actions, attitudes and words reflect His love. As the children experience your love, they can more readily understand and accept God's love. Help them to know God made them and loves them. Help them to know Jesus as a kind, loving friend.

Wherever a child goes, he takes all of himself. He takes a child who is fearfully and wonderfully made; a child who grows in his own way and at his own rate—just as God has planned.

KINDERGARTNERS

PHYSICAL GROWTH

Kindergartners are physically active. They enjoy large muscle activities. They are rapidly developing skill in using their bodies, legs and arms. Although they are less restless than at four, they need exercise. Provide opportunities for bodily movement through activities using large muscles such as dramatic play, block building, finger fun and action songs that require jumping, stretching and bending.

Encourage freehand drawing with large crayons. Provide clay or salt/flour dough for the child to use. Alternate active and quiet experiences so children are not required to sit still for more than four or five minutes. Keep furnishings to a minimum, allowing open space for moving about. Provide a fenced, out-of-door space for regular periods of play each day. Provide safe equipment—large balls, ropes, digging equipment and a sand box.

While the child's growth rate is slowing, girls are maturing more rapidly than boys in their physical development. Both boys and girls are improving in their small muscle control. They use their fingers efficiently now; however, do not expect them to color accurately within lines. Also, cutting accurately is still difficult for some fives.

Most five-year-olds are learning to write (print). Praise their accomplishments. However, be careful not to embarrass the child who is not yet able to write. Find other areas in which he or she can receive equal praise. Avoid comparing children to each other.

MENTAL GROWTH

Kindergartners' attention spans are still limited. Do not expect them to sit quietly for long periods. During Together Time provide a variety of lesson-related activities in which they can have a part; change activities frequently. Offer several Bible learning activities during each lesson. Expect children to move from one to another.

When you tell a story use visual resources to sustain children's interest. Use action words such as *run, walk* or *climb*. Change the inflection of your voice to create feelings of excitement, weariness, happiness, etc. Occasionally whisper to create a quiet mood. "The wind howled. The big waves crashed against the little boat. Then, Jesus said, 'Be still!' The wind stopped howling. The waves stopped crashing (whisper) and everything was calm and still."

Kindergartners are curious and eager to learn. They learn rapidly and ask many questions. Answer their questions simply in ways that will stimulate their own thinking. Never tell children what they can find out for themselves.

Five-year-olds still rely on their senses for most of their learning. Use objects they can see, touch, smell, taste and hear. Provide many opportunities for activities which are within their ability. Be sensitive enough to step in when help is needed, but not to interfere when a child is able to complete a task successfully.

Five-year-olds interpret words literally; they do not understand symbolic concepts. Use words that mean exactly what they say. Avoid symbolic ideas, such as "sunbeams for Jesus" or "ask Jesus into your heart." These are confusing to children.

EMOTIONAL GROWTH

Kindergartners need affection and security. They rely on consistent and dependable adult supervision. They find security in knowing what is expected of them. They need limits. Establish a routine with which they can become familiar. Keep materials in the same locations so the children know where they can be found.

Children seek affection from other children and adults. They are anxious for adult approval and want to establish a good relationship with their teacher. Give the child individual attention. Listen closely when he talks to you. Let him know with a smile, a word of praise, a hug or a pat on the shoulder that he's special to you.

Kindergartners like to help. By helping they receive the approval and attention they need and seek. Helping tasks, such as distributing materials and picking up scraps also help children work off some of their excess energy. Give them responsibilities which they can perform successfully. Praise them when they complete a task.

SOCIAL GROWTH

Kindergartners enjoy working in small groups. Plan activities to be done with two to five children. During Bible learning activities let children choose the group in which they will work. Encourage conversation among the children in small groups. Provide adult help to insure that every child can be involved.

SPIRITUAL GROWTH

A kindergartner thinks of God in a personal way. A five-year-old can sense the greatness, wonder and love of God only when these concepts are expressed in specific and familiar terms. For instance, simply telling the child, "God made the world," is not nearly so meaningful as displaying nature objects for the child to examine. Then words like "God made everything in our world, even these beautiful shells," take on real significance.

Children can think of the Lord Jesus as a friend who loves and cares for them. Jesus' love must be interpreted in specific terms—by helping children know that the Lord Jesus expresses His love and care through their families.

Kingergartners have a simple trust in God. They are ready to accept all you tell them of God and the Lord Jesus. It is imperative that a teacher's information be accurate and be expressed as simply as possible. Even more important is that the gospel of God's love becomes real as children feel love from adults. Teachers who demonstrate their faith in a consistent, loving way become channels through which God can be made known to young children.

PRIMARIES (1st and 2nd Graders)

PHYSICAL GROWTH

The child of six or seven is going through a period of decreased physical growth, while coordination and muscle control are improving steadily. Writing begins to be legible and cutting is becoming accurate. The term "constant motion" describes the behavior of sixes and sevens. Expect wiggling and squirming. Plan appropriate activities in which the child may be a *doer of the Word and not a hearer only* (see Jas. 1:22). Provide frequent changes of pace, and build in plenty of opportunity for physical movement.

MENTAL GROWTH

An intense eagerness to learn is a delightful and extremely important characteristic of first and second graders. They ask innumerable questions and frequently try to answer them through experimentation and discovery. Even though their attention span is short, they enjoy repetition. Familiar stories and activities can be very meaningful. They are primarily interested in the here and now, rather than in the past or future. Their listening and speaking vocabulary is well developed, and reading skill increases by leaps and bounds. Most second graders enjoy activities that require some reading skills. It is important to plan learning activities that will encourage the eagerness present at this point in the child's life.

Sixes and sevens still think in literal terms. Avoid symbolism. Use plenty of visual illustrations.

EMOTIONAL GROWTH

First and second graders are still bound to home, but at the same time adventuring out into a strange and sometimes confusing world. Making decisions sometimes is difficult. They seek independence but often must be very dependent.

Make sure every child you guide knows and feels that you love him or her. Express your affection and show your interest in every child as an individual.

SOCIAL GROWTH

First and second graders are still deeply concerned about receiving adult approval while struggling to become socially acceptable to other children. The concept of, *Do for others what you want them to do for you* (see Luke 6:31) is a difficult one to accept. Being first and winning are very important at this age. However, these children are becoming capable of accepting the opinions and wishes of others and of thinking about the welfare of the total group.

Six- and seven-year-olds need the warm, supportive, understanding friendship of adults in order to find their places in group situations. The child needs to value himself as a person and then to value each individual within the part of the world he knows. A child's social growth process involves a movement from "I" to "you" to "we."

SPIRITUAL GROWTH

Six- and seven-year-olds are able to sense the greatness, wonder and love of God when these concepts are expressed in specific terms within children's experience. For example, teach about God as creator by displaying nature objects that children can examine. They understand that God sent His Son, Jesus, as an expression of His great love. They begin to understand how Jesus can change lives. Sixes and sevens begin to use the Bible as their reading skills increase. They are able to grasp more and more the greatness of God's love as revealed in Bible stories and as teachers point out specific acts of love in class and in family life.

This is a time to help children develop confidence and skills in prayer. Prayer needs to become a natural expression of gratitude and petition. Each child can understand that God, in His wisdom, will decide upon the best answer to his prayers. Each child can talk to God anywhere, anytime, and in his own words, thus experiencing the importance of prayer in his daily life.

It is of the utmost importance that sixes and sevens develop strong values that will build a foundation for the years to come. Understanding and feeling are vital stepping-stones to the application response in the daily lives of children. Workers in this department are a very important link in helping children to translate their feelings of love for God into visible responses. They need to help children find concrete ways to show God's love to others. It is not enough to merely talk about it.

MIDDLERS (3rd and 4th Graders)

PHYSICAL GROWTH

Physically, the eight- and nine-year-olds are in a period of steady growth. Coordination is well enough developed to allow them to react with speed and accuracy. Development of the muscular system permits longer attention span. They enjoy adequate energy, much enthusiasm and enough self-confidence to permit them to be active participants in projects which capture their keen interest.

MENTAL GROWTH

Communication skills of third and fourth graders develop at a rapid rate. Individual differences among children result in widely varying rates of progress. Both eight- and nine-year-olds are interested in using their newly developed reading skills to read portions of the Bible. They want to know more about Bible characters. They seem to constantly question adults.

The middler's interest span widens as he is exposed to more experiences. His concepts of time, space and distance are increasing. He is able to relate to the past and to the future, as well as to the present.

Creative art and drama both provide valuable learning experiences. The expression of thoughts and feelings through art and drama help the middler work through problem situations and internalize Bible information, both of which will encourage him to exhibit Christian behavior.

Gradually the middler realizes that there may be more than one answer to a question, more than one idea about a given subject, and more than one opinion in a discussion. He is willing to listen to ideas presented by adults, as well as those from his peer group. He enjoys looking up information and discovering his own answers to problems and questions.

Middlers memorize easily; teachers must make sure these children *understand* as well.

EMOTIONAL GROWTH

Third and fourth graders are sometimes torn between the need to be a child and the desire to be grown up. They are building a strong sense of fair play and a value system that distinguishes between right and wrong.

Eight- and nine-year-olds increase in ability to be independent in making choices. They become increasingly aware of the larger world and show concern with the rights and feelings of others. They often express a strong curiosity about faraway places in the world. This is an excellent opportunity for involvement in the missionary program of the church.

SOCIAL GROWTH

As the desire to have status within the peer group becomes more intense, dependence upon adults decreases. Loving, understanding guidance of adults provides essential support as children struggle with disagreements and problems with their peers in self-directed group activities.

Even though the child is working for group approval, it seems to be important that he or she have a special friend of the same sex. Activities and interest are also heavily dependent upon the same sex at this age.

Through the process of working, playing and living with the peer group, middlers test their own limitations and skills. Self-image depends greatly on achievements compared with those of peers. The desire for acceptance strongly motivates the child to participate in group activities. A cooperative project can be planned and carried through with real enthusiasm and success. This is an ideal time to include church-related group activities or clubs into the total plan of the church.

SPIRITUAL GROWTH

Learning to make choices and decisions based upon recognition of right and wrong is important for eight- and nine-year-olds. Sometimes it is difficult to admit wrongdoing. Adults can encourage middlers to understand the loving, forgiving nature of God. Adults also need to help satisfy middlers' needs to forgive others.

The prayer life of eight- and nine-year-olds is one of honesty, simplicity and trust. They can realize that God stands ready to help and will hear their prayer at any time. It is sometimes difficult for children of this age to know that God's answer to prayer is best, even when it is not answered in just the way they might want it to be. Understanding that God is an all-wise, all-knowing, all-powerful and loving God can become a part of the child's beliefs and feelings.

Many eights and nines can understand what it means to need Jesus as their personal Saviour. Children who indicate an awareness of sin and a concern about accepting Jesus as Saviour need to be carefully guided without pressure. Opportunities to experience trust, love, sorrow and forgiveness in their daily life will help children to understand and accept the love and forgiveness of God.

JUNIORS (5th and 6th graders)
PHYSICAL GROWTH

Ten- and eleven-year-old children are healthy and full of energy. Motor control is well developed, enabling them to participate in many "doing" activities with enthusiasm and success.

Both ten- and eleven-year-olds are active, curious, enthusiastic, honest and creative. They are interested in the world about them. They seek to experience a wide variety of things which are new and different.

Ten-year-old boys and girls are usually about the same height. Many eleven-year-old girls start a physical growth spurt which causes them to be taller than boys at the same age. Eleven-year-old boys are often restless and wiggly in comparison to the more mature girls. Children of this age may tire easily because of physical changes.

MENTAL GROWTH

Fifth and sixth graders are generally very verbal. Talking, questioning and discussing need to be utilized in the teaching-learning plan. Concrete examples and specific information are still easier for these learners to deal with than abstract or symbolic concepts and generalizations. They can think through situations and arrive at logical conclusions. Ten- and eleven-year-olds continue to be creative persons. They are able to express ideas and feelings through poetry, songs, drama, stories, drawing and painting. They can use roleplaying as a means of working out problems.

Juniors are anxious to know the reasons for right and wrong. Making ethical decisions is a challenging task. They begin to question adult concepts, wanting to determine things independently. Adult guidance must be available, but given in such a way that it will not destroy the children's efforts in becoming thinking, self-directed persons.

Ten- and eleven-year-olds will work for long periods of time with concentration and enthusiasm on projects that are interesting and have meaning for them. They will often go far beyond the expectations of adults. Are you providing for choices of activities which will be interesting and vital? It is important that juniors be encouraged to learn Bible truths through involvement, action and discovery. Provide opportunities for meaningful application to daily living. Tens and elevens can easily absorb Bible facts. But learning is not complete unless these facts can be translated into daily action. Caring leaders and teachers can bring about this necessary carry-over, through careful guidance of learning experiences.

EMOTIONAL GROWTH

Ten-year-olds have reached an emotional balance which allows them to be happy with themselves. As a result, they are generally cooperative, easy going, content, friendly and agreeable. Most adults enjoy working with this age group. Ten-year-olds may evidence feelings of anger, but are quick to return to their happy selves. Even though both girls and boys begin to think about their future as adults, their interests tend to differ at this point.

Adults need to be aware of behavioral changes in many eleven-year-olds. They experience unsteady emotions and often shift from one mood to another. They move quickly from sadness, dejection and anger, to happiness. Adults frequently observe indications of jealousy or fear. All of these emotions are a part of the journey from childhood to adulthood. These changes of feelings require patient understanding from the adults in their world. Juniors need to be able to make choices and decisions within the necessary limits that are set by peer groups or adults.

SOCIAL GROWTH

Juniors have several centers for social activities. They are concerned with family relationships, and the values, judgments and feelings of their parents. They want to be involved with their brothers or sisters in family excursions and projects. Juniors also value their peer group quite strongly. They like to be a part of the group, and do not want to stand apart for any reason. Their ability to make valuable contributions to group activities is a beneficial experience for them. They can participate happily and with success in groups beyond the family cluster, and are interested in maintaining the group code of behavior. Because of their desire to gain status within the peer group, many will readily compete with others. Competition is even more intense when the group is involved in a contest, especially with a group of the opposite sex. This is all a part of their need to find a place in their world.

Eleven-year-olds often become increasingly critical of adults and unwilling to communicate with them. They may make unrealistic demands for independence.

SPIRITUAL GROWTH

Juniors are capable of deep feelings of love for God and an appreciation of God's love for them. They can be aware of their need for God's forgiveness and their need for a personal Saviour. They can experience a closeness with God through prayer and Bible reading, and often seek to share their faith with their peer group. They are developing a sense of responsibility to the church. This may include the desire to be present for worship, to accept some responsibility for work within the church, or to be involved in service projects.

This is an ideal time to encourage Bible reading. Fifth and sixth graders can use the Bible independently. Looking to God for guidance through Bible study is within their capability.

They can use Bible study tools, such as a concordance, Bible dictionary, commentary, and other related resource materials. Guidance in the selection and use of such study materials is important to help them use the Bible to answer questions, to help with problems, and as a Bible learning activity.

Tens and elevens bring increased skill, reasoning, and a widening background of experience to Bible learning activities. It is important to help tens and elevens use basic Bible facts to build a framework for understanding how the Bible relates to daily life.

YOUTH

What can the adult expect from a young person at any given age? How does the junior high differ from the senior high? What can one expect from a class of eighth graders? Or twelfth graders?

The goal of the adolescent is to find an identity. He or she wants an answer to the question, "Who am I?" Related to this search for identity is the problem of self-acceptance and acceptance by peers.

SEVENTH GRADERS

Rapid change marks the life of twelve-year-olds, especially the girls. Many girls are a full year ahead of most boys in physical and social development. Those boys who do mature early tend to become early leaders. Both girls and boys desperately want to be a part of the crowd. Self-esteem depends primarily on acceptance by the group.

Seventh graders show rapid maturation in their thinking. Whereas the facts of the story satisfied them before, now they want to know *why*. They start to think abstractly. Principles begin to take on a new meaning, for they are able to understand them as a form of thought. They begin to test the facts they have previously accepted. They may experience questions and doubts. But these elements are just emerging; many traces of childhood still linger.

EIGHTH GRADERS

Then comes eighth grade. The girls continue to grow at a rapid rate during this year, with many boys beginning to surge but still lagging behind. Thirteen-year-olds are cautious. It almost seems as though they go into a period of hibernation until they feel they can cope with themselves and with other people. Their rate of growth leads to an increase in insecurity and concern over acceptance.

Mentally, they become very reflective. As they turn inwardly, largely due to the physical changes they are undergoing, they also start working through some of the new insights they are able to grasp. As they work through these ideas, they are on their way to developing a perspective on life. Their peers continue to exert great influence, as do older youth. However, eighth graders look for leaders to follow and to imitate—all part of their search for their own identity.

NINTH GRADERS

Suddenly, they are in the ninth grade, and what a difference! They feel almost grown up. They have new eagerness to express themselves as they find they can communicate their feelings. Ninth-graders' security increases so they can open up again to the outside world. Girls begin to develop womanly proportions, and the boys start to notice.

Ninth graders feel far removed from the world of seventh and eighth graders. Yet many schools and churches continue to group them together. The ninth graders frequently have leadership qualities, but they tend to get impatient with the "childish" interests and behavior of their younger peers.

TENTH GRADERS

The tenth grade is often called the fifteen-year-old-slump. Again the adolescent turns inward.. For many boys this is a year of rapid growth, and the often embarrassing voice change. They seem so overwhelmed by the changes taking place within that they simply retreat inside a shell and attempt to sort things out. They appear to have an air of indifference. They are unsure of themselves, and find it much safer to pull in and shut out the rest of the world.

The adult can be of most help to this age group by simply being available when needed, and serving as a sounding board to the young people's questions and ideas. It is a time of ups and downs as well as a time of changing interests. What holds their attention today will bore them tomorrow. So the understanding ear of the adult will listen with patience and understanding. Conversely, the prying adult will only shut off communication.

The gap between youth and adults is often at its widest point at age fifteen. It begins to widen around age twelve. From this point it grows rapidly to its largest gap at age fifteen. Fifteen-year-olds are not just older fourteen-year-olds. They are more pre-sixteen-year olds. They do not look back, except to pull things together for the big push towards adulthood.

ELEVENTH GRADERS

Beginning at age sixteen, the gap starts to close until around age twenty-two, when the former adolescents are part of the adult world. Sixteen marks their entrance into the pre-adult stage. They are becoming *self-reliant* as they feel that they have passed the major part of the journey through adolescence. Even adults treat them as though they were almost one of them.

Along with this comes a feeling of independence, heightened by the new status and freedom of a driver's license. The eleventh graders are not fighting for independence anymore—they are using it. This gives them a growing feeling of self-assurance as they are finding themselves as persons and starting to like what they find. Since they feel more comfortable with themselves, they are able to develop a new quality in their relationships with the opposite sex. They develop meaningful friendships, although the girls take them more seriously than the boys do. They have their problems, but generally age sixteen is still "sweet sixteen."

TWELFTH GRADERS

From seventeen onward, the road smooths out. Teenagers realize that they are on the threshold of adulthood—that childhood and adolescence are almost things of the past. This realization points them toward decisions concerning the future. What next? Vocation now or college? What about marriage? They are increasingly aware of people and issues beyond themselves. Parents take on a renewed importance as the seventeen-year-olds feel more comfortable with them. They develop the ability to be involved in mature study and leadership positions both in society and within the church. Again, these are generalizations. There will be many exceptions. In fact, one whole group at a particular age level can be an exception. A ninth grade class may be quiet and withdrawn, like the eighth graders are supposed to be.

Since growth is a progression, we resist the tendency to put our ninth graders in the "ninth grade box." Instead, we try to find out why they are at a different point in the growth pattern than expected. Perhaps they are at a tenth-grade level—the fifteen-year-old slump. This might be due to the presence of several strong leaders among the class who have pushed the others in their development. Or, they might be at the eighth grade level due to the lack of any strong leaders in the group.

Adults learn about teens by observation—listening to their discussions, talking with them, reading their written work. We find out whether they are at the eighth grade or tenth grade level by observing their relationships with and attitudes toward the opposite sex. If they are behind, the sexes will sit on opposite sides of the room. If they are ahead of schedule, the boys will be interested in the girls. They may be lingering in childhood in the way they think and act, as the eighth-grader does, or straining toward the goal of adulthood, as the tenth-grader will be starting to do.

Youth today do not simply worship without understanding. If something is sacred, then there must be a valid reason why it is sacred. Spontaneous discussions are an important element of the youth culture. Time fades in importance as the discussion grows and deepens in intensity. These events are what life is all about. This is where learning takes place.

These are difficult years because of the shift from dependence to independence. Adolescence is a time of *preparation* for independence, not of actual independence. The young person is eager to be free, but still is not quite ready to accept all the responsibility that independence requires. Junior highs are tossed about by this conflict. One moment they are asserting their independence, the next moment they seek the reassurance that they can still depend on mom and dad. These fluctuations will lessen as adults give youth opportunities for responsibility as they move on through senior high school.

"Praise youth and it will prosper" is a proverb to remember as you work with young people. People tend to live up to your expectations. If you show a lack of confidence in a young person, his or her self-confidence will be shaken, thus hindering personal growth and spiritual maturity.

You can encourage your students by asking them for their viewpoint. Then listen attentively to what they say. Show interest in their ideas by making comments or asking questions. Let them know you appreciate their participation. Be ready with sincere words of praise. Follow up praise with warmth and friendliness. This is an important part of teaching. As psychologist William Glasser says, "If you examine why you succeeded with a kid, you'll find out you first succeeded in making friends with him."

ADULTS
COLLEGE AGE

College age adults are generally considered to be eighteen (or a high school graduate) to about twenty-three years old. College age adults may or may not be in college. If not, they may be working. Working people and students often live in two different worlds and associate with different types of people.

Even so, people this age do have many things in common. Most of them are trying to establish their sexual identity, to learn sex roles, and to become close to others. They struggle with questions of career choices, finances, and possibly marriage. They may be rebellious as they assert their independence, getting away from the authority of parents and others, launching themselves on a life of their own.

YOUNG ADULTS

Young adults (ages 24-35) are independent, and they're searching for something new, different, and better than what they have so far experienced. They choose their own values and experience a new freedom. They are asking, "Who am I?" "Where am I going?"

Young adults have important decisions to make—finding a mate, choosing a career, having children. They need help and guidance from the Christian community in all these areas. And, having made the decision, having gotten married, taken a job, given birth to a child, they need help in living with these decisions. They need to learn how to live as a marriage partner and parent, how to serve God as a working person. Those who choose to remain single, or to marry but not have children, also need guidance and support in their life-styles.

Young adults must learn to manage a home, live on their income, feed their families nutritious meals on a limited budget. They need to learn to avoid the time-payment trap. They need to learn basic principles of Christian stewardship.

Young adults need social contacts with others who have similar interests and experiences. The church can provide this setting for social contact.

MIDDLE ADULTS

Middle adults cover a large age span—from 35 to 60 or 65 years old. But try telling anyone who's 35 or even 45 that he or she is middle aged! Perhaps middle adulthood is a better term.

Like so much of life, middle adulthood is a time of transition and stress. People get older and less attractive. Children grow up and become those mystifying and terrifying creatures, teenagers. Then they grow up even more and go to college, acquire jobs, get married, have children. Suddenly the "middle adult" has to face up to being a middle-aged grandparent! Or, if child-bearing has been postponed, the "early middle" adult couple may face a "now or never" feeling about starting a family. The never-married may be coming to terms with facing the rest of life alone. The divorced and widowed have shattering adjustments to make.

Many middle adults reach the peak of their earning power during middle age. They may be prominent and successful, or stuck in unexciting jobs, with no hope for a better future. They feel too old or too defeated to make a change—and indeed, society is not kind to anyone over forty who is looking for a job. Some middle adults take on extra jobs. Many wives work, either for the money or for a sense of personal fulfillment or both.

Middle adults come to realize that their lives are established. They have reached their goals or they have not. They may not have much chance of reaching youthful goals, and so they may be frustrated if they cannot accept the need to change those goals to more attainable ones. Even Christians can be joyless, powerless, and gloomy. They deeply need the help of the church to revitalize their lives.

Middle adults need fulfilling leisure time and social activities. They need to find areas where they can give of themselves as they are capable. They need continued guidance in husband-wife and family relationships (remember they have those teenage children!) or in coping with living as singles. (Perhaps a refresher course in dating?) As they get older they need much warmth and reassurance that they are still valuable persons in God's scheme, in the church's planning, and in their family's view.

Middle adults may also be facing problems and decisions regarding their own parents. They may face questions of extended nursing care, where the parents should live (with the middle-aged children?), and other factors that may put additional stress on the parent-child relationship.

OLDER ADULTS

Older adults (ages 60 and up) face an accelerating aging process. They face retirement and possibly a much reduced income. They face the deaths of their friends and loved ones, and the impending event of their own death. They may suffer an increasing number of physical ailments and disabilities.

Retired adults may lose their sense of usefulness. They lose one of their most consistent sources of being with people. They may suffer actual economic want.

Older adults often feel that all their friends are dying. And when a loved one—especially the spouse—dies, many adjustments must be made. Older adults need a loving and wise ministry from the church at this time.

Despite the problems, however, older adults can be active and alert. They have more time for hobbies, travel (if they can afford it), social pursuits and Christian service. An effective ministry will provide older adults with a variety of activities, to which they can invite their unchurched friends.

Older adults may learn more slowly, but they can still learn. Now that they have more time, they may be able to devote themselves to Bible study more than ever before. And, in turn, they may be able to teach others, work with children and young people, share their skills with younger adults.

As you work with adults, realistically assess their needs and their abilities. Don't pass by their potentials for service—and don't overlook the areas in which they need to be ministered to.

Chapter 16

Leading a Child to Christ

**FOR LEADERS OF PREKINDERGARTNERS
(ages three and four)**

Prekindergarten children can understand the Scripture truth that the Lord Jesus is their loving friend and helper. They are also capable of feeling genuine affection for Jesus and a desire to please Him.

Children need to hear of Jesus' love and to feel His love demonstrated in ways they can understand. The child's response to this love is the first step toward a truly lasting commitment to the Lord.

Since young children are responsive and loving, the question of leading the child to Christ must be approached with great sensitivity and with the guidance of the Holy Spirit.

**FOR LEADERS OF KINDERGARTNERS
(ages five and six)**

Some kindergarten children, particularly those who receive Christian nurture at home, may respond to Jesus as personal Saviour. Many, however, do not grasp the meaning of salvation by faith in the Lord Jesus Christ. Young children need to be able to discuss this matter individually with an understanding adult. The adult needs to ask questions to check the child's understanding, but avoid symbolic phrases ("Ask Jesus to come into your heart").

Teachers must be sensitive to the guidance of the Holy Spirit in leading a young child to Christ. For unless God Himself is speaking through His Spirit to the child, there can be no genuine heart experience.

FOR LEADERS OF PRIMARIES, MIDDLERS
AND JUNIORS (grades one through six)

The age at which children grasp the meaning of personal salvation depends on their training and background. Some boys and girls, especially those from Christian homes, will be ready to receive Jesus Christ as Saviour and Lord earlier than others. Pray that the Holy Spirit will give you wisdom and make you sensitive to every child's spiritual need.

Remember that salvation is a supernatural work of the Holy Spirit. Unless God Himself is speaking to the child, he or she cannot become a child of God.

Boys and girls can easily be influenced to follow the group. Therefore, avoid group decisions. Rather, plan for personal counseling and pray individually with any child who is ready to trust the Lord Jesus Christ as Saviour.

Use this simple presentation (From *God Wants You to Be a Member of His Family...and Grow as His Child;* see "Resources.") to explain that God wants the child to be a member of His family.

God wants you to know how to become His child. Do you know that God loves YOU? He does! God wants you to be in His family. God's Word says, "God is love" (1 John 4:8).

You and all the other people in the world have done wrong things—like stealing and cheating and telling lies and not believing in Jesus. The Bible word for doing wrong is sin. God says that you have sinned and that sin must be punished. God's Word says, "All have sinned and fall short of the glory of God" (Rom. 3:23).

God loves you so much He sent His Son Jesus Christ to die on the cross for your sin. Because Jesus never sinned, He is the only one who could take the punishment for your sin. God's Word says, "Christ died for our sins according to the Scriptures" (1 Cor. 15:3).

In the Bible many Scripture verses tell us that God, the heavenly Father, sent His Son Jesus to be the Saviour. God's Word says, "The Father has sent his Son to be the Savior of the world" (1 John 4:14).

Are you sorry for your sin? Tell God now that you are sorry. Do you believe Jesus died to be your Saviour? Tell God that you do believe. If you are sorry, and if you do believe—God forgives all your sin. Do you know what happens when God forgives you? He makes everything all right between you and Him. Now you are a child of God. God's Word says, "As many as received Him to them He gave the right to become the children of

God, even to those who believe in His name" (John 1:12, *NASB*).

As a child of God you receive God's gift of everlasting life. This means God is with you now and forever. "For God so loved the world, that He gave His only begotten Son, that whoever believes in Him should not perish, but have eternal life" (John 3:16, *NASB*).

FOR LEADERS OF YOUTH AND ADULTS

Your Bible ministry can prepare people and give them opportunities, as the Holy Spirit leads, to receive Jesus Christ as Saviour. Teachers need to be sensitive to the spiritual understanding of each one and be ready to talk with him individually according to his needs. The following presentation clearly explains salvation in terms a non-Christian can understand. (From *Smile, God Loves You;* see "Resources.")

SMILE! GOD LOVES YOU!! Here are Four Things He Wants YOU to Know...

Ever feel empty, like nobody really cares? Well, God cares! He knows all about you and He sends you this message...

1st thing: God's goal for you is ABUNDANT LIFE! God really loves you and wants to give you the abundant life—a life full and satisfying! God's Word, the Bible, says: "For God so loved the world, that he gave his only begotten Son, that whosoever believeth in him should not perish, but have everlasting life" (John 3:16, *KJV*). "...I am come that they might have life, and that they might have it more abundantly" (John 10:10, *KJV*).

What keeps most people from experiencing the abundant life?

2nd thing: Man's hang-up is SEPARATION BY SIN. God made man with a free will. Man chose to reject God's love and to disobey God. This disobedience, called sin, separates man from God. Today man still chooses to disobey. The Bible says: "For all have sinned and come short of the glory of God" (Rom. 3:23, *KJV*). "For the wages of sin is death (separation from God)" (Rom. 6:23, *KJV*).

Man has failed to solve the sin hang-up, but God has the solution.

3rd thing: God's solution is JESUS CHRIST. The ONLY solution to the sin hang-up is Jesus Christ. When Jesus Christ died on the cross in our place, He paid the penalty for our sin. He bridged the gap between God and man. "God is on one side and all the people on the other side, and

Christ Jesus, himself man, is between them to bring them together" (1 Tim. 2:5, *TLB*). "But God commendeth [shows] his love toward us, in that, while we were yet sinners, Christ died for us" (Rom. 5:8, *KJV*). "Jesus saith unto him, I am the way, the truth, and the life: no man cometh unto the Father, but by me" (John 14:6, *KJV*).

Christ doesn't force Himself upon man. Man must choose whether or not to receive God's solution.

4th thing: Man's response is RECEIVE CHRIST. You must personally invite Christ into your life and trust Him as Lord of your life. Jesus says: "Behold, I stand at the door, and knock: if any man hear my voice, and open the door, I will come in to him..." (Rev. 3:20, *KJV*). "But as many as received him, to them gave he power to become the sons of God, even to them that believe on his name" (John 1:12, *KJV*).

Is there any reason why you cannot receive Jesus Christ right now? What to do:

1. Admit that you are a sinner.
2. Be willing to turn away from sin.
3. Believe that Jesus Christ died for you.
4. Ask Him in prayer to enter and control your life.

How to pray: Simply talk honestly to God. God knows what your desire is, and He is not too concerned about the words you use. If the prayer below says what you want to say, then pray it right now: "Lord Jesus, I confess that I'm a sinner. I need help with my hang-ups. I believe that you died for ME and I receive you right now. Come into my life and take control. Help me become the kind of person you want me to be. Thank you for loving and forgiving me."

Did you really mean what you just prayed? Do you believe that your sins are forgiven and that Jesus has entered your life? "Behold, I stand at the door, and knock: if any man hear my voice, and open the door, I will come in to him" (Rev. 3:20, *KJV*). "He that hath the Son hath life; and he that hath not the Son of God hath not life. These things have I written unto you that believe on the name of the Son of God, that ye may know that ye have eternal life, and that ye may believe on the name of the Son of God" (1 John 5:12, 13, *KJV*).

Give your follow-up coordinator, pastor or Sunday School teachers the names of those who make decisions. See the chapter, "Following-Up and Evaluating" for suggestions on how to nurture your new convert.

Part V

Appendix

RESOURCES

DAY CAMPING

Counselor's Guide for Day Camping (Forest Ranger). Convention Press.

Day Camp Director's Package (Forest Ranger). Convention Press.

Fundamentals of Day Camping. Grace L. Mitchell. Association Press.

So You Want to Start a Day Camp. American Camping Association.*

FAMILY CAMPING

Church Family Camps and Conferences, rev. ed. Elizabeth and William Genne. Judson Press.

Enjoying the Outdoors with Children. Lucille E. Hein. Association Press.

Family Camping—Five Designs for Your Church. United Methodist Church. A guidance resource for leaders who plan for church-sponsored family camping. Describes five different styles of family camping: cluster, colony, camporama, caravan, and family-life conferences.

Family Life Today. G/L Publications. A monthly magazine of ideas to help families establish and maintain a Christian life-style.

Family Values Workshop. Lois Curley and Georgiana Walker. G/L Publications.

Growing Together: Child, Parent and Church. Gail B. Hanson. G/L Publications.

Heaven Help the Home. Howard G. Hendricks. Victor Books. Offers a plan of operation for the effective family that turns out durable, functional, and winsome people to represent Jesus Christ in a stormy age.

How to Begin Family Camping in the Church. Robert H. Helmkamp. Christian Camping International.**

How to Succeed in Family Living. Clyde M. Narramore. Regal Books.

Now That I'm a Christian (Basic Steps to Growth). vols, 1, 2. Chuck Miller. Regal Books.

You, the Parent. Lawrence O. Richards. Moody Press.

YOUTH CAMP

God Wants You to Be a Member of His Family . . . and Grow as His Child. G/L Publications.

God Wants You to Know How to Live as His Child. G/L Publications.

Resources for Youth Mini-Camps. Success With Youth. Detailed plans for youth mini-camps, conferences, retreats and seminars; for weekend camps or all-day events. Ecology retreat, survival hike, witness strategy seminar; retreats built around Scripture themes and planning conferences. Bible study outlines, menus, recreations ideas and other features.

Smile, God Loves You (Here Are Four Things He Wants You to Know). G/L Publications.

SENIOR CITIZENS

Adventures with Older Adults in Outdoor Settings. George B. Ammon. Pilgrim Press.

SPECIAL CAMPING

Camping for Special Children. Thomas M. Shea. C. V. Mosby, Co. Order from Christian Camping International**

Camping with Retarded Persons. United Methodist Church. Finding and training leaders, facilities, organization and administration.

Your Camp and the Handicapped Child. Dr. Phyllis M. Ford. American Camping Assocation. For director and counselor in a camp that has one or more handicapped persons attending.

CAMP ADMINISTRATION AND COUNSELING

Campcraft Instructor's Manual. American Camping Association.* Following the philosophy that successful outdoor living is dependent upon certain knowledge, skills and attitudes acquired only through actual experience in progressive stages, this manual provides the instructor with a framework for a successful program for campers of all ages and abilities.

A Guide to Church Camping. John LaNoue. Convention Press.

A Notebook for the Christian Camp Counselor. John LaNoue. Convention Press.

An Introduction to Christian Camping. Werner Graendorf and Lloyd Mattson. Moody Press.

Help . . . I'm a Camp Counselor. H. Norman Wright. Regal Books.

Planning Outdoor Christian Education. Ronald K. Johnson. Pilgrim Press. An administrative guide for planners of outdoor experiences with older elementary girls and boys. Includes content, program, purpose, settings, buildings, characteristics of the children, what makes a good leader, stewardship of the enviroment.

CAMP GAMES, CRAFTS, CREATIVE ACTIVITIES

Bible Word Search. William C. Gordon. Baker Book House. Delightful, informative and entertaining collection of word puzzles on Bible themes. Useful rest hour pastime for campers, rainy-day project, helpful teaching tool for cabin study.

Celebrate. Pennsylvania Council of Churches. Songs, games, poems and ideas to be shared either by the family or by any camping group. Order through American Camping Association.*

Craft Digest. Follett Publishing Co. The techniques of 25 different crafts are described and comprehensively illustrated.

Crafts from Plastic Cast-Offs. Standard Publishing Co.

Creative Craft Ideas for All Ages. Edited by Shirley Beegle. Standard Publishing Co.

Creative Crafts for Self-Expression. Sarah Howell. Broadman Press.

Easy-to-Make Crafts (For Children, ages 3-11). Compiled by Dolores Rowen. Regal Books.

Easy-to-Make Crafts (For preteens and youth). Compiled by Dolores Rowen. Regal Books.

Easy-to-Make Puppets and How to Use Them—Early Childhood.

Easy-to-Make-Puppets and How to Use Them—Children and Youth. Fran Rottman. Regal Books.

Fun Plans for Church Recreation. Agnes Durant Pylant. Broadman Press.

Games and Parties for All Occasions. James W. Kemmerer and Eva May Brickett. Baker Book House. Games and activities for camps.

Indoor/Outdoor Recreation Pack. Broadman Press.

Learning About Nature Through Crafts. Virginia W. Musselman. Stackpole Books. Directions for creating 150 useful, decorative or just-for-learning projects from things easily found anywhere in nature's storehouse. Order through American Camping Association.*

Learning About Nature Through Games. Virginia W. Musselman. Stackpole Books. All in fun, campers learn to identify animals, birds, trees, flowers. Order through American Camping Association.**

Let's Go Outdoors with Children: Administration Guide for Grades 1-4. Richard and Betty Purchase. Westminster Press. Discusses age-level characteristics and interests of younger elementary children (grades 1-4) and how to plan for these in outdoor experiences.

Outdoor Arts for Kids. Charleen Kinser. Follett Publishing Co. All of the projects in the book use readily available materials and were designed and executed by youngsters themselves. Chapters on sand casting, weaving, snow sculpture and ice molds, mud art, mosaics, wind toys, handmade musical instruments and bundled grass figures.

Puppet Scripts for Use at Church. Edited by Everett Robertson. Broadman Press.

Using Crafts Activities in the Church. Bob Sessoms. Convention Press.

Using Puppetry in the Church. Edited by Everett Robertson. Broadman Press.

158 Things to Make. (Crafts for Young Children). Compiled by Margaret M. Self. Regal Books.

301 Creative Crafts. Standard Publishing Co.

STUDY RESOURCES

Creative Bible Learning for Adults. Monroe Marlowe and Bobbie Reed. Regal Books.

Creative Bible Learning for Children Grades 1-6. Barbara J. Bolton and Charles T. Smith. Regal Books.

Creative Bible Learning for Young Children, Birth-5 Years. Donna Harrell and Wesley Haystead. Regal Books.

Creative Bible Learning for Youth, Grades 7-12. Ed Reed and Bobbie Reed. Regal Books.

Emotions: Can You Trust Them? Dr. James Dobson. Regal Books.

Ethel Barrett Tells Bible Stories to Children, vols. 1 and 2. Ethel Barrett. Regal Books.

Ethel Barrett Tells Favorite Bible Stories. Ethel Barrett. Regal Books.

Families Go Better with Love. Howard Hendricks. Victor Books. Cabin devotions.

Family Life Today. G/L Publications. A monthly magazine of ideas to help families establish and maintain a Christian life-style.

Good Morning, Lord: Devotions for Boys. William C. Hendricks. Baker Book House. Sixty-one-page devotionals concluding with a thought, a challenge or a prayer. A helpful book for boys' counselors.

How People Learn. International Center for Learning, G/L Publications.

"How to Use Your Bible" Cards in three packets: *What's in the Bible? What's in the Epistles? How to Use Your Bible.* G/L Publications.

Recruit . . . Train . . . Plan. International Center for Learning, G/L Publications

Science and the Bible . . . Can We Believe Both? Larry Richards. Victor Books.

MUSIC

The Good Times Songbook. Compiled by James Leisy. Abingdon Press. 160 songs for informal singing—sacred, folk, traditional; good resource for camps and retreats. Guitar chords and melody score.

Sing 'n Celebrate for Kids; Sing 'n Celebrate, vols. 1, 2. David C. Cook.

NATURE LORE/CONSERVATION

Ecology. Shelly and Mary L. Grossman. A How and Why Wonder Book by Grosset and Dunlap, Inc. Discusses the chain of life; habitat; seasons and biometry.

A Leader's Guide to Nature-Oriented Activities. Betty van de Smissen and Oswalk H. Goering. Iowa State University Pres. Program and teaching activity for camps.

Look What I Found. Marshall Case. Chatham Press. Ways to enjoy constructive experiences by discovering the fascinating animal world around us. Order through American Camping Association.*.

Nature Walk. Janet Clark, Mary Alice and Gary Collins. Burgess Publishing Co. Order from Christian Camping International.**

Teaching in the Outdoors. Donald R. Hammerman and William M. Hammerman. Burgess Publishing Co. Order from Christian Camping International.**

Tips and Tricks in Outdoor Education, 2nd ed. Edited by Malcolm D. Swan. Interstate Printers and Publishers. A compilation of notes from the Department of Outdoor Education, Northern Illinois University.

INTERGENERATIONAL STUDY

Extended Family: Combining Ages in Church Experience. Lelia Hendrix. Broadman Press. `

Family Ministry. Leon Smith. Discipleship Resources. Contains a chapter on intergenerational study.

The Family Together: Intergenerational Education in the Church School. Sharee and Jack Rogers. Acton House, Inc.

Family Values Workshop. Regal Books. A five-session intergenerational curriculum.

A Patchwork Family. Mark and Mary Frances Henry. Broadman Press.

FOREIGN LANGUAGE MATERIALS

For Spanish materials, send request for a catalog or information to: Spanish Materials, Baptist Book Store, 4024 Montana St., El Paso, TX 79903.

FILMS AND FILMSTRIPS

For films to rent, request listings from: *Film User's Guide,* Ken Anderson Films, Box 618, Winona Lake, IN 46590; Films, Incorporated, 5589 New Peachtree Rd., Camblee, GA 30341; Insight Films, 17575 Pacific Coast Highway, Pacific Palisades, CA 90272; Mass Media, 2116 N. Charles St., Baltimore, MD 21218; Pyramid Films, Box 1048, Santa Monica, CA 90406; Swank Motion Pictures, Inc., 201 S. Jefferson Ave., St. Louis, MO 63166; TeleKETICS, Franciscan Communications Center, 1229 S. Santee St., Los Angeles, CA 90015; Twyman Films, Inc., 329 Salem Ave., Dayton, OH 45401.

Free films on topics including conservation, the arts, etc. Association Films, Inc., 866 Third Ave., New York, NY 10022. Free films can often be obtained from local social agencies, public libraries, Bell Telephone Company, government agencies, insurance companies, a local military base, a local university or college, and from the Audio-Visual Library Distribution, Eastman Kodak Co., 343 State St., Rochester, NY 14650.

Filmstrips: *Uncovering Christians: Student Work in Mexico; Campers on Mission; Ready to Go: Mission Youth Groups.* Broadman Press.

Recruiting Is Everybody's Job. International Center for Learning.

* American Camping Association, Bradford Woods, Martinsville, Indiana 46151.
**Christian Camping International, Box 400, Somonauk, Illinois 60552.

BIBLE MINISTRIES
COUNTDOWN SCHEDULE

20 Weeks Before
- Set dates.
- Appoint director and co-director.
- Announce in church bulletin dates, type and location of ministry (day camp, backyard Bible school, etc.), and names of director and co-director.
- Order VBS Review Kit and filmstrip for review.
- Pray; also ask church groups to pray.

18 Weeks Before
- Appoint a department leader, secretary and craft coordinator for each age group; also, missions, publicity, finance, supplies, refreshment, transportation coordinators.
- Meet with department leaders to:
  1. Outline recruitment schedules.
  2. Set deadline dates for all activities.
  3. List all staff needs.
  4. Compile lists of prospective workers.
  5. Order lesson materials (use last year's attendance reports for guide).
- Plan missions project with missions coordinator.
- Plan Training Workshops.

16 Weeks Before
- Meet with department leaders for prayer.
- Begin recruiting procedures (see "Recruiting Your Staff").
- Put announcements in church bulletin.

14 Weeks Before
- Distribute VBS or other ministry theme buttons to all staff members. Ask them to be "VBS Boosters" and wear the buttons at church.
- Select teaching staff
- Give materials to department leaders.
- Plan publicity with publicity coordinator.

12 Weeks Before
- Insert special flyer (or other ministry promotion) in church bulletin.
- Meet with department leaders for prayer.
- Plan dedication service for workers; secure pastor's approval and help.
- Plan a rally for preregistration and orientation.
- Plan closing program to present to parents and community.
- Plan follow-up program with Sunday School leaders.
- Order all supplies not previously ordered.

11 Weeks Before
- Arrange display of teaching materials and crafts in foyer.
- Emphasize in the church bulletin the need for workers—give names of department leaders as "persons to see."

10 Weeks Before
- Complete recruiting of all prospects.
- Director, co-director meet with department leaders to work out Training Workshop procedure. Discuss the overall goals and aims for your Bible ministry and the individual department aims.

9 Weeks Before
- Announce in church bulletin beginning of Training Workshops. (Assure all volunteers that they will receive practical, helpful training and guidance.)
- Director and/or co-director contact all recruits, confirming preliminary assignments.

8 Weeks Before
- Begin publicity.
- Recheck staff and materials. (Be sure all responsibilities are assigned, materials are received and workers are preparing.)
- Staff prayer meeting. (Pray for staff, preregistration.)

7 Weeks Before
- Send follow-up letter to all staff members recruited thus far, reminding them of the Training Workshops. Bulletin announcements emphasize Training Workshops.

6 Weeks Before
- Director and co-director meet with department leaders for final review of staff:
  1. Are all staff positions filled?
  2. Are all staff assignments confirmed?
  3. What prospects are left for unfilled positions?
- Send final reminder card on Training Workshops.
- Begin Training Workshops!

4 Weeks Before
- Training Workshops continue.
- Check with coordinators (missions, publicity, finance, supplies, refreshments, transportation) to determine if they are accomplishing their assignments.
- Staff prayer meeting. (Pray that your ministry will have eternal results.)
- Dedication of workers (approximately one week before your ministry).

- Conduct rally and preregistration.
- Check and adjust time schedules.

During Bible Ministry

- Pray with and for your staff regularly.
- Maintain spirit of enthusiasm and encourage workers.
- Secure additional supplies as needed.
- Visit departments; make necessary adjustments.
- Have someone available to run errands.
- Make sure secretarial records are being properly kept.
- Direct the closing program.

After your Bible ministry

- Thank the Lord for His blessing. (Pray for the follow-up program. These are the fruits of your Bible ministry.)
- Express appreciation to all workers.
- Begin follow-up program. (See "Following-Up and Evaluating.)
- See that supplies are packed, labeled and stored for next year.
- File names and addresses of workers to be contacted next year.
- Make written notes of all good ideas for next year. Note how problems were solved and how to avoid similar problems.
- Be sure coordinators' reports are completed. (Include notes of necessary adjustments in schedules, additional supplies needed, etc.)

SAMPLE PERMISSION FORM

_____

Date

_____ has my permission to attend
Student's name

_____ at _____
Name of program   Location

from _____ to _____

_____

I give my permission for him/her to be transported to _____
location

and back to _____
location

I also give my permission for him/her to have whatever emergency medical treatment is necessary.

My child has the following allergies or special diet, or requires the following medication (which I will provide) at the stated times: _____
_____
_____
_____

_____
Signature of parent or guardian